意外に面白い！簡単に理解できる！
英語対訳で読む日本の歴史

中西康裕 Yasuhiro Nakanishi 監修
Gregory Patton 英文監訳

JIPPI Compact

実業之日本社

装幀／杉本欣右
本文まんが／あおむら純
DTP／ユニックス
本文執筆・編集／中堂良紀（マイプラン）

PREFACE

The purpose of this book is to read Japanese history with simple English.

In general, most of us have few opportunities to read English sentences in our everyday lives. There may be many people who think they need perfect knowledge of English to read long English sentences, and they may not want to read English while checking a dictionary. But, without such knowledge, you can read English sentences whose content you are familiar with because you know the subject matter in advance. This book deals with Japanese history that you learned when you were in elementary school or in junior high school. With this book, you can review the Japanese history you have already learned and you can study English as well! You can kill two birds with one stone!

In this book, every English and Japanese sentence is numbered and it is easy to compare English with Japanese. By doing so, you can review Japanese history and study English. Many English words and phrases are underscored and explained in Japanese, which will help you with reading difficult sentences.

Native speakers of English, Japanese children returning from English speaking countries and so on can also learn Japanese history with this book. We also recommend this book very highly to people who are interested in Japanese history and are also good at English.

In this book, you can learn special terms used in Japanese history only by reading English. For example, we carefully describe the special terms like '*Daijo-daijin* (grand minister of state)', so you will read them and learn how to pronounce the terms in Japanese and their English meanings at a glance. This book will be more fun when you read it with interest in how to express in English those special terms used in Japanese history.

Isn't it cool to say, "I'm reading Japanese history in English"?

I'd like to express special thanks to the supervising editor, Prof. Nakanishi Yasuhiro, Mr. Gregory Patton, the staff at MYPLAN for editing, the staff at UNIX for DTP, and Mr. Ogino Mamoru of Jitsugyo no Nihon-sha. Ltd.

The writer ／ Nakado Yoshiki of MYPLAN

はじめに

　本書は日本史を平易な英語で読むための本です。
　一般に，私たちは日常生活の中で英語の文章を読む機会がそれほど多くありません。英語の長文を読むためには英語の完璧な知識が必要だと考えている方々も多いかもしれませんし，そういった方々は辞書を引きながら英語を読みたいとは思わないかもしれません。しかし，そのような知識がなくても，親しみのある内容の英文なら，読むことができるでしょう。何が書いてあるのかあらかじめ知っているのですから。本書は小学校や中学校で私たちが学んできた日本史を取り上げています。かつて学んだ日本史のおさらいをしながら，英語の学習もできるのです。そんな，一冊で二度おいしいのが本書なのです。
　すべての英文，和訳文にそれぞれ番号をつけて，英文と和訳文を対応しやすくしてあります。そうすることで，日本史のおさらいと英語の学習ができます。また，英単語や語句の多くに下線を引いて，日本語の説明をつけました。それはわかりにくい英文を読むときのヒントとなるでしょう。
　英語を話す外国の方や日本人の帰国子女には，本書で日本の歴史を学んでもらうことができます。そのほか，日本史に興味のある英語が得意な方々にもとてもオススメです。
　また，英語を読むだけで日本史用語を学ぶことができるようにしました。たとえば，「太政大臣」は「*Daijo-daijin*(grand minister of state)」と表記して，日本語の読みと英語の意味が一目でわかるようにしています。「日本史に出てくるあの用語は英語で何というのだろう？」と興味・関心を持って読んでいただくと，本書をより楽しめると思います。
　「日本史を英語で読んでいるんだ」なんて，ちょっとかっこよくありませんか？
　監修をしていただいた中西康裕先生，Gregory Patton先生，編集をしていただいたマイプランのみなさん，DTP(デスクトップ・パブリッシング：コンピュータで雑誌や書籍などの出版物のデザイン作成やレイアウト設定をすること)をしていただいたユニックスのみなさん，そして実業之日本社の荻野守さんに，この場を借りて厚く御礼申し上げます。

執筆／マイプラン　中堂良紀

Contents
目 次

Contents

Chapter 1

The Ancient Times ~From the Birth of Japan to the Time of Nobles
古代 日本の誕生から貴族の世の中

1. The Birth of the Japanese Islands — 12
   日本列島の誕生
2. Jomon Culture — 14
   縄文文化
3. Yayoi Culture — 16
   弥生文化
4. A Lot of Small States — 18
   小国の分立
5. The Queen of Yamatai State, Himiko — 20
   邪馬台国の女王卑弥呼
6. Ko-fun and Yamato State (Ancient Burial Mounds and Yamato State) — 22
   古墳と大和政権
7. Torai-jin (Immigrants from the Korean Peninsula) — 24
   大陸文化を伝えた渡来人   Introducing the Continental Culture
8. The Government of Prince Shotoku — 26
   聖徳太子の政治
9. Asuka Culture — 28
   飛鳥文化
10. The Reformation of Taika — 30
    大化の改新
11. Jinshin Disturbance — 32
    壬申の乱
12. The Birth of Ritsu-Ryo State — 34
    律令国家の成立
13. Heijo-kyo — 36
    平城京
14. The Changing of Land System — 38
    土地制度の移り変わり
15. Tempyo Culture — 40
    天平文化
16. Heian-kyo — 42
    平安京
17. The Sekkan Government — 44
    摂関政治
18. Kokufu Culture — 46
    国風文化

Column Snake ~ The Gods That Are Disliked — 48

Contents

Chapter 2

The Middle Ages ~The Time of Samurai, the Time of Wars
中世 武士の時代、争乱の時代

19. The Growth of Samurai and the Local Revolts —————— 50
    武士の成長と地方の反乱
20. The Insei (The Rule by the Cloistered Emperors) —————— 52
    院政
21. The Hei-shi Administration ————————————————— 54
    平氏の政権
22. The Taira-Minamoto War ————————————————— 56
    源平の合戦
23. The Kamakura Shogunate ————————————————— 58
    鎌倉幕府
24. The Shikken Government and Jokyu Disturbance —————— 60
    執権政治と承久の乱
25. The Goseibai-shikimoku and the Life of Samurai —————— 62
    御成敗式目と武士の生活
26. The Dual Control and the Life of Peasants ————————— 64
    二重の支配と農民の生活
27. The Mongol Invasion ————————————————————— 66
    元の襲来
28. Kamakura Culture ————————————————————— 68
    鎌倉文化
29. The New Government of Kemmu ————————————— 70
    建武の新政
30. The Disturbance of the Northern and Southern Court ——— 72
    南北朝の動乱
31. The Muromachi Shogunate ————————————————— 74
    室町幕府
32. The Kango Trade ————————————————————— 76
    勘合貿易
33. The Development of Industry and Economy ——————— 78
    産業と経済の発達
34. The Formation of the Soson ————————————————— 80
    惣村の形成
35. The Self-governing by the Ikki ————————————— 82
    一揆による自治
36. The Onin War ————————————————————— 84
    応仁の乱

Contents

37. The Gekokujo and the Warring Lord —— 86
下剋上と戦国大名

38. The Development of the Cities and the Town People —— 88
都市の発展と町衆

39. Muromachi Culture —— 90
室町文化

Column Dog ~ The Fact Dog-lovers Don't Want to Know —— 92

Chapter 3 The Modern Ages ~The Unification of Japan and the Rise of Common People
近世 天下統一と庶民の台頭

40. The Arrivals of Guns and Christianity —— 94
鉄砲とキリスト教の伝来

41. The Rise of Oda Nobunaga —— 96
織田信長の台頭

42. Oda Nobunaga's Ambition to Unify Japan —— 98
織田信長の天下統一事業

43. The Honno-ji Temple Incident —— 100
本能寺の変

44. Toyotomi Hideyoshi's Unification of Japan —— 102
豊臣秀吉の全国統一

45. Hideyoshi's Diplomatic Policy and Sending Army to Korea —— 104
秀吉の対外政策と朝鮮出兵

46. Momoyama Culture —— 106
桃山文化

47. The Battle of Sekigahara —— 108
関ヶ原の戦い

48. The Establishment of the Edo Shogunate —— 110
江戸幕府の成立

49. The System of the Rule by the Edo Shogunate —— 112
江戸幕府の支配のしくみ

50. The Shuin-sen Trade (The Vermilion-Seal Certificate Trade) and the Japanese Towns —— 114
朱印船貿易と日本町

51. The Ban on Christianity and the National Seclusion —— 116
禁教と鎖国

52. The Three Capitals: Edo, Osaka and Kyoto —— 118
三都~江戸・大坂・京都

53. The Government by Tokugawa Tsunayoshi and the Shotoku-no-chi —— 120
徳川綱吉の政治と正徳の治

54. Genroku Culture —— 122
元禄文化

Contents

55. The Reform of Kyoho —— 124
享保の改革
56. The Government by Tanuma Okitsugu —— 126
田沼意次の政治
57. The Reform of Kansei —— 128
寛政の改革
58. The Change in Farm Villages, Ikki and Uchikowashi —— 130
農村の変化と一揆・打ちこわし
59. The Access of Foreign Ships —— 132
外国船の接近
60. Kasei Culture —— 134
化政文化
61. The Reform of Tempo —— 136
天保の改革

Column Horse ～Too Sophisticated? —— 138

Chapter 4 The Present Age ～Japan in the International Community
近代 国際社会の中の日本

62. The Perry's Arrival —— 142
ペリー来航
63. The Unification of the Court and the Shogunate, —— 142
公武合体と尊王攘夷　　and the Imperialist's Antiforeigner
64. The Satsu-Cho Allaiance and the To-baku Movement —— 144
薩長同盟と討幕運動
65. The Return of Power Back to the Emperor and the Restoration —— 146
大政奉還と王政復古
66. The Boshin War —— 148
戊辰戦争
67. The Meiji Restoration —— 150
明治維新
68. Nation's Wealth and Military Strength —— 152
富国強兵
69. Civilization and Enlightenment —— 154
文明開化
70. The Seikan-ron and the Seinan War —— 156
征韓論と西南戦争
71. The Movement for Democratic Rights —— 158
自由民権運動
72. The Constitution of the Empire of Japan and the Imperial Diet —— 160
大日本帝国憲法と帝国議会

Contents

73. The Treaty Revision —————————————————— 162
    条約改正
74. The Japanese-Sino War ————————————————— 164
    日清戦争
75. The Japanese-Russo War ———————————————— 166
    日露戦争
76. The Battle of Tsushima ————————————————— 168
    日本海海戦
77. The Annexation of Korea ————————————————— 170
    韓国併合と日本の産業革命　and the Industrial Revolution in Japan
78. Modern Cultures ———————————————————— 172
    近代の文化
79. World War I and Japan ————————————————— 174
    第一次世界大戦と日本
80. The War Boom and the Rice Riot ——————————— 176
    大戦景気と米騒動
81. The Taisho Democracy ———————————————— 178
    大正デモクラシー
82. The World Crisis and the Response of the Countries ——— 180
    世界恐慌と各国の対応
83. The Manchurian Incident ———————————————— 182
    満州事変
84. The Withdrawal from the League of Nations —————— 184
    国際連盟脱退
85. The Rise of the Military and the Japanese-Chinese War —— 186
    軍部の台頭と日中戦争
86. The Reinforcement of War Footing ———————————— 188
    戦時体制の強化
87. Germany and World War II ——————————————— 190
    ドイツと第二次世界大戦
88. The Outbreak of the Pacific War ———————————— 192
    太平洋戦争勃発
89. The Wartime Life of the People ————————————— 194
    戦時下の国民生活
90. The Potsdam Declaration and the End of the Pacific War —— 196
    ポツダム宣言と太平洋戦争の終結
91. Postwar Japan ————————————————————— 198
    戦後の日本

Chapter 1
The Ancient Times

From the Birth of Japan
to the Time of Nobles

第1章 古代
日本の誕生から貴族の世の中

1. The Birth of the Japanese Islands

① About one million years ago, the Earth entered the ice age. ② Large animals like Naumann's elephants and mammoths were living in Japan at that time because Japan was part of the continent. ③ People caught those elephants using chipped stone tools. ④ They lived behind rocks and used fire. ⑤ The period when people used chipped stone tools is called the Old Stone Age.

⑥ About ten thousand years ago, the ice age was over and the Japanese Islands were cut off from the continent by a rise in sea level. ⑦ It is said they were almost the same shape as now.

⑧ We now think that our oldest ancestor was Australopithecus, who lived about four million years ago. ⑨ They walked upright on two legs and made chipped stone tools.

⑩ Java man and Peking man came into being five hundred

12

thousand years ago and the Neanderthal, two hundred
thousand years ago. ⑪Forty or fifty thousand years ago
appeared Cro-Magnon, who is our direct ancestor. ⑫We
can find from their cave paintings that Cro-Magnon
made stone tools, hunted and fished.

1. 日本列島の誕生

①今から約100万年前、地球は**氷河時代**に入りました。②このころ日本列島は大陸と地続きでナウマンゾウやマンモスなどの大形の動物が住んでいました。③人々は**打製石器**をつけたやりなどを使ってナウマンゾウなどをつかまえていました。④人々は簡単な小屋や岩かげなどに住み、火を使って暮らしていました。⑤このように打製石器を使って、狩りや採集をしていた時代を、**旧石器時代**と呼びます。

⑥今から約1万年前、氷河時代が終わると、海水面が上昇し、これまで大陸の一部であったところが島となりました。⑦それはほぼ現在と同じ形だったようです。

⑧現在知られている最古の人類は、今から約400万年前に生きていた**アウストラロピテクス**とされています。⑨彼らは2本足で直立して歩き、打製石器をつくり使用していました。⑩約50万年前には**ジャワ原人**、**ペキン原人**、約20万年前には**ネアンデルタール人**と呼ばれる人類があらわれました。⑪約4〜5万年前には、現在の人類の祖先にあたる**クロマニョン人**があらわれました。⑫彼らが住んでいた洞くつの壁画から、石器をつくり狩りや漁を営んでいたようすを知ることができます。

2. Jomon Culture

①An earthenware culture was born when the Japanese Islands were cut off from the continent about ten thousand years ago. ②This earthenware has patterns of rope on the surface, so we call it *Jomon* ware. ③The period from about ten thousand years ago to about the 4th century B.C.(before Christ) is called the *Jomon* period. ④As people came to be able to cook with the earthenware, their food life was enriched.

⑤People started to grow plants in this period, but agriculture was not developed. ⑥They lived by hunting, fishing and gathering. ⑦They made pit houses and lived in them on the waterfront where it was easy to get something to eat. ⑧Shell mounds, where they threw out the bones of animals and seashells, were formed near those colonies. ⑨They also made clay figures that are called *dogu*. ⑩Most of them were modeled on women and they were used to keep off evil spirits and to pray for the rich supply of food. ⑪There seems to have been no gaps between the rich and the poor and no differences in social standing because all the dead were buried equally in the shell mounds or in mass graves.

2. 縄文文化

①約1万年前に日本列島ができたころ、土器を使う文化が生まれました。②この土器は表面に縄目の文様がつけられることが多いため**縄文土器**と呼ばれています。③約1万年前から紀元前4世紀ごろまでを**縄文時代**といいます。④縄文時代には、土器を用いてものを煮たきできるようになり、食生活は以前より豊かになりました。

⑤また縄文時代には、植物の栽培が始まりましたが、農耕はあまり発達しませんでした。⑥人々は狩りや漁や採集で生活していました。⑦人々は食料が得やすい海岸や水辺に**竪穴住居**をつくって住みました。⑧集落の近くには、動物の骨や貝がらなどをまとめて捨てた**貝塚**ができました。⑨また、**土偶**と呼ばれる人形もつくられました。⑩土偶は女性の姿をかたどったものが多く、魔よけや食物の豊かさを祈るのに使われました。⑪縄文時代には、人々が貝塚や共同墓地に平等に葬られている様子から、貧富の差や身分の違いは存在していなかったと考えられています。

3. Yayoi Culture

① In the 4th century B.C., rice farming was first introduced to northern *Kyushu* by people from the continent. ② It spread to eastern Japan quickly. ③ Metalware was also introduced to Japan. ④ There were swords, pikes, mirrors and bells made of bronze. ⑤ The swords and the pikes were used not only as weapons but also as treasures for festivals. ⑥ Ironware was used as weapons but it was also used to make wooden farm tools, axes and rowboats.

⑦ When rice farming and metalware were introduced, people began to make high-quality auburn earthenware. ⑧ This earthenware is called *Yayoi* ware. ⑨ The period from the 4th century B.C. to the 3rd century A.D.(of the Christian Era) is called the *Yayoi* period.

⑩ Rice farming changed the structure of society very much. ⑪ People settled around rice paddies and formed their own underline{communities}. ⑫Among them appeared a leader who underline{managed} their underline{teamwork}. ⑬underline{Rich-poor gaps} seem to have arisen in this period.

リーダー、有力者　管理した　　　　　　共同作業　　　　　　貧富の差
（むら）

---

3. 弥生文化

①紀元前4世紀ごろ、大陸から渡来した人々によって、**稲作が**伝えられました。②稲作は、まず九州北部に伝わり、急速に東日本にまで広まりました。

③金属器も日本に伝わりました。④青銅器には、銅剣・銅矛・銅鏡・銅鐸などがありました。⑤銅剣や銅矛は武器としても使われていましたが、主に祭りのための宝物として用いられました。

⑥鉄器は、武器に使われたほか、木製の農具やおの、そして舟などをつくる工具としても使われました。

⑦稲作や金属器が伝わったころ、赤褐色の上質の土器がつくられるようになりました。⑧この土器は**弥生土器**と呼ばれました。⑨弥生土器が使われた紀元前4世紀から紀元後3世紀ごろまでを**弥生時代**といいます。

⑩稲作の開始によって、社会のしくみは大きく変化しました。⑪人々は水田のまわりに定住して、むらをつくりました。⑫むらの中には、共同作業の中心となる有力者があらわれました。⑬このころから貧富の差も出てきたと考えられています。

4. A Lot of Small States

①In the *Yayoi* period, communities quarreled about water and land that was suitable for rice farming. ②The leaders of those communities later became thanes or kings.
③In the quarrels, powerful communities defeated other ones and ruled them, and they grew to be small states. ④In this way, a lot of small states which kings or thanes ruled were formed.
⑤In history books of China, Japan around the era was called *Wa* and there were more than 100 small states. ⑥Some of them sent emissaries to China. ⑦The king of the state, *Na-no-kuni*, in *Wa* sent emissaries to Houhan in the 1st century and he was given a gold seal by the Emperor. ⑧A gold seal inscribed with *Kan-no-wa-no-na-no-kokuou* was found in the island, *Shika-no-shima*, and it is said to be this seal.

⑨The Chinese history book, *Gishi-wajin-den*, says

that there was a state named *Yamatai* state and its
邪馬台国

queen *Himiko* ruled more than 30 small states. ⑩ She
女王卑弥呼

sent emissaries to the capital of Wei and was given the
魏の都(Weiは魏の中国名)

title of *Shin-gi-wa-ou*.
~という称号　親魏倭王

4．小国の分立

①稲作が広まった弥生時代の社会では、稲作に適した土地や用水をめぐって、むらとむらの間に争いが起こりました。②むらの有力者は、やがて人々を支配する豪族や王へと変わっていきました。

③むら同士の戦いの中で、勢力の強いむらは周辺のむらを従えて、小さなクニへ成長していきました。④このようにして、王や豪族の支配する小国が数多く存在するようになりました。

⑤中国(漢)の歴史書からは、紀元前後の日本は倭と呼ばれていて、100余りの小さな国があったことを読みとることができます。⑥その中には中国に使いを送った者もいたと記されています。⑦1世紀中ごろには、日本の奴国の王が後漢に使いを送って、皇帝から金印を与えられたという記録もあります。

⑧志賀島(福岡県)で「漢委(倭)奴国王」という文字が刻まれた金印が発見されており、このときの金印であろうといわれています。

⑨『魏志』の倭人伝には、日本に邪馬台国という国があり、女王卑弥呼が倭の30余りの小さな国々を従えていたと記されています。⑩また、卑弥呼は使いを魏の都に送り、魏の皇帝から「親魏倭王」という称号を授かったことも記されています。

5. The Queen of Yamatai State, Himiko (邪馬台国の女王卑弥呼)

Wa! Wa!

2世紀後半の倭では争いが絶えず、邪馬台国でも戦いが続きました。

Call me the Queen.
女王様とお呼び。

そこで、卑弥呼が邪馬台国の女王になりました。

Send emissaries to Wei.
魏に使いを送りなさい。

All right.
はは〜

Got it?
わかったか？

卑弥呼は占いやまじないが得意で、神のお告げにより政治をすることができました。

卑弥呼は人前には姿を見せず、卑弥呼の弟が彼女の言葉を人々に伝えました。

第1章 古代●日本の誕生から貴族の世の中

239年、卑弥呼は使いを送りました。

魏の皇帝からは「親魏倭王」の称号と金印、銅鏡などが授けられました。

邪馬台国のことは『魏志』の倭人伝に記されていますが、いまだに邪馬台国があった場所は謎であり、北九州説と畿内(大和)説があります。

卑弥呼が亡くなると、邪馬台国は再び乱れました。

卑弥呼の娘、壱与(台与)を立てて、争いがおさまりました。

6. Ko-fun and Yamato State (Ancient Burial Mounds and Yamato State)

①In the late 3rd century, a powerful state was born around *Yamato*. ②This state is called *Yamato* state and its government is called the *Yamato* Court. ③It was a government with a king at its center and was made up of powerful thanes in *Kinki*. ④The king of the *Yamato* Court ruled the kings from *Kyushu* to southern *Tohoku* in the 5th century and was called the great king.

⑤In this period, powerful kings and thanes were buried in large tombs covered with large mounds of earth. ⑥This kind of tomb is called *Ko-fun*. ⑦*Daisen Ko-fun* in *Osaka* is as long as 486 meters and one of the world's largest. ⑧This style of burial mounds is called *Zenpo-koen-fun* (keyhole-shaped tomb mound). ⑨It started being used mainly in *Yamato* in the late 3rd century, and it came to be used all over the country. ⑩They entombed bronze mirrors and iron weapons in

the *Ko-fun* as well as the dead body. ⑪Clay figures
called *Haniwa* were put around *Ko-fun*.

~だけでなく　遺体
はにわ　置かれた

6. 古墳と大和政権

①3世紀後半ごろ、大和(奈良県)を中心とする地域に強力な国が生まれました。②この国を大和国家、その政府を大和朝廷と呼んでいます。③大和朝廷は、王を中心にして、近畿地方の有力な豪族によってつくられていました。④大和朝廷の王は、5世紀には九州から東北地方南部までの各地の王を従えて、大王と呼ばれるようになりました。

⑤このころ、有力な各地の王や豪族は、土を高く盛り上げてつくった大きな墓に葬られるようになりました。⑥このような墓を古墳といいます。⑦大阪府にある大仙古墳は、全長が486mもある世界最大級の墓です。⑧形は前方後円墳です。⑨前方後円墳は、3世紀後半に大和を中心につくられはじめ、各地でもつくられるようになりました。⑩古墳には遺体とともに銅鏡や鉄製の武器などが納められました。⑪古墳のまわりには、はにわと呼ばれる焼き物が置かれました。

7. Torai-jin (Immigrants from the Korean Peninsula) Introducing the Continental Culture

① In the 4th century, there were conflicts between the north and south of China. ② On the Korean Peninsula, Goguryeo unified the northern part and became powerful. ③ Baekje and Silla came into being in the southern part. ④ *Yamato* state expanded into the Korean Peninsula. ⑤ According to the Chinese history book, *So-jo*, five kings of *Wa* sent emissaries to the Southern Court of China. ⑥ The five kings tried to be recognized as the kings of *Wa* and to be allowed to rule the southern part of the Korean Peninsula.

⑦ *Wa* came to have close relationships with the states on the Korean Peninsula and many people immigrated into *Wa* from there. ⑧ These people are called *Torai-jin*. ⑨ They introduced the superb culture of the continent such as farming techniques. ⑩ They also taught the techniques of raising silkworms and making cloth and the earthenware, *Sue-ki*. ⑪Chinese characters, Confucianism and Buddhism were introduced, too. ⑫*Yamato* state used the knowledge and techniques of the *Torai-jin* to strengthen its hand.

---

7. 大陸文化を伝えた渡来人

①4世紀ごろ、中国では南と北に分かれて国々が対立していました。②朝鮮半島では、高句麗が北部を統一して勢力をのばしました。③南部では百済と新羅がおこりました。④大和国家は朝鮮半島に進出しました。⑤『宋書』には、倭の五王(大和国家の大王)が、中国の南朝に何度も使いを送ったという記述があります。⑥倭の王としての地位と朝鮮半島南部を支配する地位を認めてもらおうとしていたのです。

⑦朝鮮半島の国々との交流がさかんになると、朝鮮半島から多くの人々が倭に渡来しました。⑧このような人々を**渡来人**といいます。⑨渡来人は、農業技術など、大陸の進んだ文化を伝えました。⑩また、養蚕や織物をつくる技術、須恵器と呼ばれるかたい質の土器を伝授しました。⑪漢字、儒教、仏教を伝えたのも渡来人でした。⑫大和国家も支配力を強めるために渡来人の知識や技術を利用しました。

8. The Government of Prince Shotoku

①At the end of the 6th century, Sui unified China and built up a powerful empire. ②At the start of the 7th century, Tang unified China in place of Sui. ③On the Korean Peninsula, Silla became more powerful in the 6th century and ruled the *Kara* area.

④In Japan, in the 6th century, powerful thanes of *Yamato* state continued to battle.

⑤Empress *Suiko* took the throne in 593 and then her nephew, Prince *Shotoku*, served as Regent. ⑥He formed a centralized system with an Emperor at its center. ⑦In this way, he wanted to survive the crisis at home and abroad.

⑧Prince *Shotoku* made the system of *Kan-i-12kai*(12 levels in officials' ranking). ⑨He also established the Constitution, *17jo-no-kenpo*, and showed the officials what to do. ⑩He sent *Ono-no-Imoko* to China as an emissary, <u>*Ken-Zui-shi*</u>（遣隋使）, with <u>a letter saying, "This is a</u>（～という内容の手紙） letter from the Emperor of the land of the rising sun to the Emperor of the land of the setting sun. How are you?" ⑪ It is said that the Emperor of Sui, <u>Yang-di</u>（煬帝）, <u>got angry</u>（怒った） to read this.

8．聖徳太子の政治

① 6世紀の末、隋が中国を統一し、強力な帝国をつくりました。
② 7世紀のはじめには隋にかわって唐が中国を統一しました。
③ 朝鮮半島では、6世紀に新羅の勢力が強くなり、加羅地方は新羅の支配下に置かれました。
④ 6世紀ごろの日本では、大和国家の有力な豪族の争いが続いていました。
⑤ 593年、女帝の推古天皇が即位すると、おいの聖徳太子（厩戸皇子）が摂政になりました。⑥ 聖徳太子の政策は天皇を中心とする中央集権のしくみを整えることでした。⑦ そうすることで内外の危機を乗り越えようとしました。
⑧ 聖徳太子は、冠位十二階の制度を定めました。⑨ さらに十七条の憲法を制定して、天皇に仕える役人の心がまえを示しました。⑩ また、小野妹子らを遣隋使として中国に派遣した際、「日の出づる国の天子が、手紙を日の沈むところの天子に送ります。お元気ですか。」と書いた国書を送りました。⑪ 隋の皇帝煬帝は、この手紙を読んでたいへん腹を立てたといわれています。

9. Asuka Culture

①After the introduction of Buddhism (仏教の伝来) from Baekje in the 6th century people were surprised at the teachings of Buddhism (仏教の教え). ②Buddhist culture flourished (栄えた) around the palace (宮) in the *Asuka* area (飛鳥地方). ③It is called *Asuka* culture. ④The temples, *Asuka-dera* temple (飛鳥寺) built (建立された) by *Soga-no-Umako* (蘇我馬子), *Shitenno-ji* temple (四天王寺) and *Horyu-ji* temple (法隆寺) built by Prince *Shotoku* are typical of (〜を代表する) this culture.

⑤The Buddha statue (仏像), *Shaka-san-zon-zo* (釈迦三尊像) at *Horyu-ji* temple is a work (作品) of *Kuratsukuri-no-Tori* (鞍作鳥) and it is similar to the sculptures of the Buddha (仏像彫刻) in China. ⑥*Kudara-kannon-zo* (百済観音像) at *Horyu-ji* temple and *Miroku-bosatsu-zo* (弥勒菩薩像) at *Koryu-ji* temple (広隆寺) are the well-known sculptures of the Buddha in *Asuka* Culture.

⑦*Tamamushi-no-zushi* (玉虫厨子) at *Horyu-ji* temple and *Tenju-koku-shucho* (天寿国繍帳) at *Chugu-ji* temple (中宮寺) are famous works of art (工芸品) as well (同様に).

⁸In *Asuka* culture, temples(寺院), sculptures of the Buddha and works of art were made mainly by immigrants(渡来人) and their descendants(子孫). ⁹Most of them received influence from the culture of the Korean Peninsula, China, India(インド) and West Asia(西アジア). ⁱ⁰*Asuka* culture was one with a rich international flavor(国際色豊かな).

9．飛鳥文化

①6世紀に百済(ペクチェ(くだら))から仏教が伝えられ、人々は仏教の教えに圧倒されました。②宮があった飛鳥(あすか)地方(奈良盆地南部)を中心に、仏教をもとにした文化が栄えました。③これを飛鳥文化といいます。

④蘇我馬子(そがのうまこ)が建立した飛鳥寺(あすかでら)(奈良県)、聖徳太子が建立した四天王寺(してんのうじ)(大阪府)や法隆寺(ほうりゅうじ)(奈良県)がこの文化を代表する寺院です。

⑤法隆寺に納められている釈迦三尊像(しゃかさんぞんぞう)は、鞍作鳥(くらつくりのとり)(止利仏師(とりぶっし))の作品で、中国の仏像彫刻の影響がみられます。⑥法隆寺の百済観音像(くだらかんのんぞう)や広隆寺(こうりゅうじ)(京都府)の弥勒菩薩像(みろくぼさつぞう)なども飛鳥文化を代表する仏像彫刻です。⑦また、法隆寺の玉虫厨子(たまむしのずし)や中宮寺(ちゅうぐうじ)の天寿国繡帳(てんじゅこくしゅうちょう)は、飛鳥文化を代表する工芸品です。

⑧飛鳥文化の寺院建築や仏像彫刻、工芸品の製作は、渡来人やその子孫が中心になって行なっていました。⑨その多くは、朝鮮半島や中国、インドや西アジアの文化に影響を受けたものです。ⁱ⁰飛鳥文化が国際色豊かな文化だったことを示しています。

10. The Reformation of Taika

①Around the middle of the 7th century, Tang attacked Goguryeo. ②Japan had to hurriedly ready for battle. ③On the other hand, after Prince *Shotoku*'s death, the *Soga* family carried out the government autocratically in the Court and people didn't like it.

④In this surroundings, in 645, Prince *Naka-no-Oe* and *Nakatomi-no-Kamatari* defeated the *Soga* family and began to reform the political system. ⑤Prince *Naka-no-Oe* wanted to form a centralized government by the Emperor. ⑥This is called the Reformation of *Taika*. ⑦On the Korean Peninsula, Silla was trying to ruin Baekje. ⑧Japan sent a large army to the Peninsula to save Baekje. ⑨But Japan lost the battle of *Hakusuki-no-e* heavily. ⑩After that, Prince *Naka-no-Oe* became Emperor *Tenji*. ⑪After his death, his brother, Prince *Oama*, and his son, Prince *Otomo*, fought for the

imperial title. ⑫Prince *Oama* defeated Prince *Otomo* in 672 in *Jinshin* Disturbance. ⑬Prince *Oama* became Emperor *Temmu*.
壬申の乱　　　　　　　　　　　　　　　　　　　　　　天武天皇

10．大化の改新

①7世紀の中ごろ、唐が高句麗を攻めました。②日本でも戦いに備える国づくりが急がれました。③一方で、朝廷では聖徳太子の死後、蘇我氏が独裁的な政治を行ない、反発が高まっていました。

④このような情勢をみた中大兄皇子は、645年に中臣鎌足(のちの藤原鎌足)らと蘇我氏を倒し、政治の改革を始めました。⑤中大兄皇子は、天皇による中央集権的な政治を目指しました。⑥この改革を**大化の改新**(乙巳の変)といいます。

⑦そのころ朝鮮半島では、新羅が百済を滅ぼそうとしていました。⑧日本は百済を救うため、朝鮮半島に大軍を送りました。⑨しかし、白村江の戦いで大敗しました。⑩その後、中大兄皇子は即位して天智天皇となりました。⑪天智天皇の死後、弟の大海人皇子と、子の大友皇子とがあとつぎをめぐって争いました。⑫672年に大海人皇子が大友皇子をやぶり、この戦いを**壬申の乱**といいます。⑬大海人皇子は天武天皇となりました。

11. Jinshin Disturbance（壬申の乱）

The next Emperor is me! 次の天皇は私だ！ / No, it's my son! いや、わが子だ！	 You're the next Emperor. おまえが次の天皇だ。
天皇の後継をめぐり、天智天皇と弟の大海人皇子は対立していました。	死の床についた天智天皇は、大海人皇子に皇位継承を告げました。
I'll retire in *Yoshino*. わ、私は吉野に引退します。	 My dear son, you're the next Emperor. 息子よ、おまえが次の天皇だ。
暗殺の危険を感じた大海人皇子は吉野に逃れました。	天智天皇は、息子の大友皇子を後継者に指名して亡くなりました。

Oh, my god.
ちくしょ〜!!

美濃 / 尾張 / 吉野

大海人皇子は東国へ向かいました。

第1章 古代●日本の誕生から貴族の世の中

Defeat Emperor *Otomo*!
大友皇子を討て〜！

Thanks!

東国の豪族たちは、大海人皇子の味方になり、近江に攻め上りました。

Defeat Prince *Oama*!
大海人皇子を討て〜！

No. It won't pay.
割りが合わないからイヤだね。

672年

Prince *Oama* triumphed!
大海人皇子の大勝利〜！

大友皇子も西国の豪族を動員しましたが、あまり集まりませんでした。

ついに672年7月、両軍が激突しました。

Indeed regrettable ...
無念だ・・・

I continued to carry out the government with the Emperor at its center.
私は天皇中心の政治をいっそう進めたのです。

大友皇子は自ら命を絶ちました。

大海人皇子は都を飛鳥に移し、673年に即位して天武天皇になりました。

12. The Birth of Ritsu-Ryo State

①*Taiho-Ritsu-Ryo* Code was enacted in 701. ②With that, they carried out the government on the basis of *Ritsu-Ryo* Code and formed the centralized system with the Emperor at its center. ③This centralized state is called *Ritsu-Ryo* state. ④The Emperor and nobles, who had been thanes in *Kinai*, played central roles in the government.

⑤In *Ritsu-Ryo* state, *Jingi-kan* (the Department of gods) and *Daijo-kan* (the Department of politics) were in the center. ⑥Under *Daijo-kan* were eight *Sho*. ⑦They placed *Koku*, *Gun* and *Ri* in the rural areas. ⑧*Kokushi*, *Gunji* and *Richo* governed their places. ⑨Land and people belonged to *Kuni* (*Kochi-komin* system). ⑩They made family registers every six years, gave people who were age six or over *Kubun-den* (the divided farm lands) and made them return the land to

to *Kuni* when they died (*Handen-shuju* system).
　　　　　　　　　　　　　　　　　　　班田収授法

⑪ There were taxes named *So*, *Cho* and *Yo*. ⑫ People
　　　　　~という名の税があった　　　　租　調　　　庸
who got *Kubun-den* had to pay *So*. ⑬ And men had
　　　　　　　　　　　　　　　　　　　　　　　　男子
to pay local specialties as *Cho* and cloths as *Yo*.
　　　　地方の特産物　　　　　　　　　　布
⑭ Moreover, men had to do hard labors such as *Zoyo*,
　さらに　　　　　　　　　　　　　　　　　　　　　　　　雑徭
Sakimori and *Eji*.
防人　　　　　　衛士

---

12. 律令国家の成立

①701年に**大宝律令**が制定されました。②これにより律令に基づいて政治を行なう国家が完成し、天皇中心の中央集権のしくみが整いました。③このような中央集権の国家を**律令国家**といいます。④天皇と貴族となった畿内の有力な豪族が中心となって政治を行ないました。

⑤律令国家では、まず中央に、**神祇官**と**太政官**の2官が置かれました。⑥太政官の下には政務を行なう**8省**がつくられました。⑦地方には国・郡・里を置きました。⑧**国司、郡司、里長**がそれぞれを治めました。

⑨土地と人民は国のものとされました(**公地公民**)。⑩そして6年ごとに戸籍をつくり、6歳以上の男女に**口分田**を与え、本人が亡くなると国に返させる**班田収授法**を行ないました。⑪税には、租、調、庸というものがありました。

⑫口分田を与えられた人々には、租が課せられました。⑬そのほか男には調として地方の特産物を、庸として布を納めさせました。⑭また**雑徭**や**防人**、**衛士**などの負担もありました。

13. Heijo-kyo

①After the structure of the *Ritsu-Ryo* state was almost
律令国家のしくみがほぼ完成すると
completed, the Court founded a new capital in *Nara* in
　　　　　　　　　　　　つくった
710 on the model of Tang's capital, Changan. ②This
　　　～にならって　　　　　　　　　　　　　長安
capital is *Heijo-kyo* and this period is called the *Nara*
　　　　　　平城京　　　　　　　　　　　　　　　　　　　　奈良時代
period.

③In *Heijo-kyo*, the streets were set out neatly in a grid
　　　　　　　　　　　　　　ごばんの目のようにきちんと整備された
from north to south and from east to west. ④The east
side of *Suzaku-oji* street was *Sa-kyo* and the west side,
　　　　朱雀大路　　　　　　　　　　左京
U-kyo. ⑤The block at the north end of *Suzaku-oji* street
右京　　　　　区画
was called *Heijo-kyu*.
　　　　　　　平城宮
⑥In the capital, some temples such as *Yakushi-ji*
　　　　　　　　　　　　　　　　　　　　　　　　薬師寺
temple and *Toshodai-ji* temple were built. ⑦People
　　　　　　唐招提寺
bought and sold local products actively in the public
　　　　　　　　　地方の産物　　　　盛んに　　　公営の市場
market: *Higashi* market and *Nishi* market. ⑧Currency,
　　　　　東市　　　　　　　　　西市　　　　　　　貨幣
Wadou-kaichin, was issued.
和同開珎　　　　　　発行された
⑨The local area was divided into many *Kuni* and
　　地方　　　　　　～に分けられた

administrative institutions were placed in each *Kuni*.
役所
⑩The governing institution, *Dazai-fu*, was established
朝廷の機関(である)　　　　　　　大宰府　　　　設けられた
in *Kyushu* and *Taga-jo* castle was established in
　　　　　　　　　　　多賀城
Tohoku. ⑪Roads were laid out from the capital to local
　　　　　　道路は整備された
areas and stations with horses were placed along them.
　　　　　馬を備えた駅

13．平城京

①律令国家のしくみが整ってくると、朝廷は唐の都長安にならって、710年に奈良に新しい都をつくりました。②この都を平城京といい、この時代を奈良時代といいます。

③平城京は、東西・南北にごばんの目のように道路が整えられました。④朱雀大路の東側が左京、西側が右京と呼ばれました。⑤朱雀大路の北のつきあたりの区画は平城宮と呼ばれました。
⑥都には、薬師寺や唐招提寺などの寺も建てられました。⑦公営の市場である東市・西市も開かれ、地方の産物などの売買が盛んに行なわれていました。⑧和同開珎と呼ばれる貨幣も発行されました。
⑨地方は多くの国に分けられ、国々には役所が置かれました。⑩九州には大宰府が設けられ、東北地方には多賀城が築かれました。⑪都と地方を結ぶ道路も整備され、馬を備えた駅が設けられました。

14. The Changing of Land System

①In *Ritsu-Ryo* state, according to the principle of *Kochi-komin*, the law, *Handen-shuju-no-ho*, was enacted. ②The burdens of *So*, *Cho* and *Yo*, and of *Ro-eki* (physical labor) and *He-eki* (military service) were so heavy that some peasants ran away. ③*Kubun-den* became in short supply because of population increase and expansion of ruined *Kubun-den* by natural disaster. ④So the government encouraged people to bring new land into cultivation.

⑤First, the government enacted *Sanze-isshin-no-ho* in 723. ⑥This was a rule that people could own the farmland for a certain fixed time if they cultivated the land. ⑦But this law was not effective because the land ruined again after the fixed time ended.

⑧Next, *Konden-einen-shizai-no-ho* was enacted in 743. ⑨This was a rule that people could own the

cultivated land forever. ⑩Nobles, temples and shrines
　　　　　　　　　永久に
made peasants cultivate new land and expanded their
　　　　　　　　　　　　　　　　　　　　広げた
private land. ⑪The principle of *Kochi-komin* had
所有地
already collapsed by the middle of the *Nara* period.
早くも崩れた

14．土地制度の移り変わり

①律令国家では、公地公民の原則のもと、**班田収授法**が実施されていました。②しかし租・調・庸や労役、兵役などの負担は重く、逃亡してしまう農民も出てきました。③さらに人口の増加と、自然の災害による口分田の荒廃のため、口分田が不足するようになりました。④そこで政府は土地の開墾を奨励しました。

⑤朝廷は、まず723年に三世一身法を制定しました。⑥これはある一定の期間、開墾した土地の私有を認めるというきまりでした。⑦しかし、私有の期限が終わると土地は荒廃し、成果は見られませんでした。

⑧そこで、743年に墾田永年私財法が制定されました。⑨これは開墾した土地を永久に私有することを認めるきまりでした。⑩貴族や寺社などは、農民を使ってさかんに土地を開墾し、私有地を広げていきました。⑪こうして公地公民の原則は奈良時代の中ごろには早くも崩れていくことになりました。

15. Tempyo Culture

①During the *Nara* period, the emissaries, *Ken-To-shi*, were sent many times and Japan had a close relationship with Tang, so culture affected by Buddhism and Tang's culture flourished in the capital. ②This is called *Tempyo* culture because it was in full flourish in the *Tempyo* era. ③Emperor *Shomu* wanted to stabilize the country by the force of Buddhism and built temples: *Kokubun-ji* temple and *Kokubun-niji* temple in each *kuni* and *Todai-ji* temple in the capital. ④He also made a large statue of Buddha for *Todai-ji* temple.

⑤Tang's priest, Jianzhen, came to Japan and worked for the development of Buddhism. ⑥*Toshodai-ji* temple and *Shoso-in* in *Todai-ji* temple are buildings that are typical of *Tempyo* culture.
⑦History books such as *A Record of Ancient Matters*

and *The Chronicles of Japan*, and the topography,
『日本書紀』　　　　　　　　　　　　　地誌
Fudo-ki, were edited in this period. ⁸The anthology, *A*
『風土記』　編集された　　　　　　　　　　　　　詩選集
Collection of a Myriad Leaves, has Japanese poems by
『万葉集』　　　　　　　　　　　　和歌
Kakinomoto-no-Hitomaro, *Otomo-no-Yakamochi*,
柿本人麻呂　　　　　　　　　　大伴家持
Yamanoue-no-Okura and so on.
山上憶良

---

15. 天平文化

①奈良時代には、遣唐使が何度も送られ、唐との交流がさかんになったため、都では仏教と唐の文化の影響を受けた文化が栄えました。②この文化は、天平年間に最も栄えたので、**天平文化**と呼ばれています。

③**聖武天皇**は、仏教の力で国を安定させることを考え、国ごとに**国分寺**と**国分尼寺**を、都には**東大寺**を建てました。④また、**大仏**をつくらせ、東大寺にまつりました。

⑤唐の僧である**鑑真**は、日本に渡来し、仏教の発展に力を尽くしました。⑥**唐招提寺**や、東大寺の**正倉院**は、天平文化を代表する建築物です。

⑦奈良時代には、『**古事記**』や『**日本書紀**』、『**風土記**』がつくられました。⑧和歌集として『**万葉集**』もつくられ、**柿本人麻呂**や**大伴家持**、**山上憶良**らの作品がおさめられています。

16. Heian-kyo

① From the late 8th century, the tug-of-war between nobles and priests became more serious, so Emperor *Kammu* embarked on political reforms. ② He moved the capital from *Nara* to *Kyoto* in 794. ③ About 400 years before the *Kamakura* shogunate is called the *Heian* period.
④ The Court often sent large armies to the *Tohoku* area and tried to rule *Emishi*. ⑤ *Emishi* raised revolt and burned *Taga-jo* castle but Emperor *Kammu* broke down *Emishi*'s resistance by appointing *Sakanoue-no-Tamuramaro* as *Seii-tai-shogun* (Barbarian Subduing General) and sending a large army.
⑥ At the start of the 9th century, *Saicho* established *Enryaku-ji* temple on Mt. *Hiei* and spread *Tendai-shu*.
⑦ *Kukai* established the *Kongobu-ji* temple on Mt. *Koya* and spread *Shingon-shu*. ⑧ In these sects,

prayers and spells called *Kajikito* (faith healing) were done. ⁹The buddhist sects which respect *Kajikito* are called *Mikkyo* (esoteric Buddhism) and they were highly valued among the imperial family and nobles.

16．平安京

①8世紀後半（奈良時代中ごろ）から、貴族と僧の間で勢力争いが激しくなったので、桓武天皇は、政治の改革に乗り出しました。②794年には、都を奈良から京都へ移しました。③この都を平安京といい、鎌倉幕府ができるまでの約400年間を平安時代といいます。

④朝廷は東北地方にたびたび大軍を送り、蝦夷を支配しようとしました。⑤蝦夷によって多賀城（宮城県）が焼かれる反乱も起こりましたが、桓武天皇は、坂上田村麻呂を征夷大将軍に任じて大軍を送り、蝦夷の抵抗をおさえました。

⑥9世紀はじめ、最澄は比叡山に延暦寺を建てて天台宗を広めました。⑦空海は高野山に金剛峯寺を建てて真言宗を広めました。⑧これらは、加持祈禱とよばれる祈りやまじないを行なうものでした。⑨加持祈禱を重んじる仏教を密教といい、皇族や貴族にもてはやされました。

17. The Sekkan Government

①*Fujiwara-no-Kamatari* (former *Nakatomi-no-Kamatari*) and his descendants had greater power than the other nobles in the *Heian* period. ②They arranged for their daughter to marry the Emperor and their baby became a new Emperor. ③From the middle of the 10th century, *Fujiwara* family members were always appointed as *Sessho* (Regent) and *Kampaku* (chief adviser). ④This government is called regency government. ⑤Regency government is at their best at the start of the 11th century. ⑥*Fujiwara-no-michinaga* and his son, *Yorimichi* were in the positions at that time.

⑦Powerful peasants in local areas went on cultivating and expanded their private land. ⑧They dedicated the land to the *Fujiwara* family and other powerful nobles and temples to protect their right to their own land.

⁹This private land is called *Sho-en* and they got
　　　　　　　　　　　　　　　　荘園
privileges like *Fuyu-no-ken* (tax exemption) and
～などの特権　　不輸の権　　　　　　免税
Funyu-no-ken (ban on admittance) over this land.
不入の権　　　　　禁止　　立ち入り
¹⁰Around the same time, local government collapsed
同じころ　　　　　　　地方の政治　　　　　　腐敗した
because most of the *Koku-shi* were keen about making
　　　　　　　　　　　　　　　　　　～に熱心だった
money.

---

17. 摂関政治

①藤原鎌足(中臣鎌足)とその子孫は、平安時代になると他の貴族をしりぞけて力をのばしました。②藤原氏は一族の娘を天皇の后にし、生まれた子を天皇にしました。③10世紀中ごろからはつねに摂政・関白に藤原氏が任命され、政治の実権を握りました。④これを**摂関政治**といいます。⑤摂関政治は、11世紀の前半に全盛となりました。⑥**藤原道長・頼通**父子のころのことです。

⑦地方の有力な農民は、開墾を進めて私有地を広げました。⑧自らの土地に対する権利を守るために、藤原氏をはじめとする有力な貴族や寺社などに土地を寄進しました。⑨このような私有地を**荘園**といい、**不輸の権、不入の権**などの特権を得ました。

⑩このころ、私腹を肥やすことに熱心な国司が多くなり、地方の政治は乱れました。

18. Kokufu Culture

①In the 9th century, Tang weakened in China and Japan stopped *Ken-To-shi* (Envoys to Tang). ②Tang went into ruin at the beginning of the 10th century. ③After a while, Sung unified China. ④On the Korean Peninsula, Silla went into ruin and Goryeo was created. ⑤From the end of the 9th century, the lifestyle of nobles was fast becoming Japanized. ⑥It is called *Kokufu* culture.

⑦Nobles lived in Japanese style houses called *Shinden-zukuri*. ⑧In art, the scenery of Japan and portraits came to be drawn. ⑨It is called *Yamato-e*. ⑩Chinese characters were changed into *Kana* ones: *Katakana* and *Hiragana*. ⑪Therefore, literature made progress. ⑫Fine stories and essays were written by women. ⑬*Murasaki Shikibu* wrote *The Tale of Genji* and *Sei Shonagon* wrote *The Pillow Book*. ⑭*Ki-no-*

Tsurayuki and others edited _Collection of Old and New Japanese Poetry_.
『古今和歌集』

⑮Around this time, the teachings of _Jodo_ became popular.
浄土信仰
⑯_Byodo-in-Ho-o-do_ temple in _Uji_ is an _Amida hall typical of this age_.
平等院鳳凰堂　　　　　宇治　　　　阿弥陀堂
この時代の代表的な

18. 国風文化

①9世紀、中国では唐の勢力が衰え、日本は遣唐使を停止しました。②唐は10世紀はじめに滅びました。③やがて宋が中国を統一しました。④朝鮮半島では新羅が滅んで高麗が建国されました。

⑤遣唐使が停止された9世紀の終わりごろから、貴族の間では生活や文化の日本化が進みました。⑥これを**国風文化**といいます。

⑦貴族は、**寝殿造**と呼ばれる住宅に住みました。⑧絵画では、日本の風景や人物が描かれるようになりました。⑨それらは**大和絵**と呼ばれました。⑩そして、漢字を変形して**カタカナ、ひらがな**のかな文字が生まれました。⑪文字が増えたことにより、文学が発達しました。⑫女性による物語や随筆などの優れた作品が登場しました。⑬**紫式部**は『**源氏物語**』を、**清少納言**は『**枕草子**』を書きました。⑭**紀貫之**らは『**古今和歌集**』を編集しました。

⑮平安時代の中ごろには**浄土信仰**が盛んになりました。⑯宇治(京都府)の**平等院鳳凰堂**は、この時期の代表的な阿弥陀堂です。

Snake
ヘビ

The Gods That Are Disliked
忌み嫌われる神

Today, snakes are hated very much. People are very scared of them and often scream at the sight of them. People sometimes throw stones at them. There was, however, some earthenware that was decorated with shapes of snakes in the *Jomon* period, and some bronze bells that had pictures of snakes drawn on them in the *Yayoi* period. It seems that ancient people had a feeling different from people today.

Japan became to have an agricultural culture because the rice cultivation reached during the *Yayoi* period. It was the water that was essential for rice cultivation. Generally, snakes like wetlands and, because of their looks, they were thought of as the children of the dragon, the god of water, or as messengers of it. Snakes came to be the symbol of religious belief as *Mizuchi* (Water Spirit).

So, various snakes appeared in ancient myths. For example, *Yamata-no-Orochi*(8-Branched Giant Snake) appeared as an evil god that interfered with agricultural work, and later, *Susa-no-O-no-Mikoto* killed it in *Izumo*. *Kusanagi-no-Tsurugi*(*Kusanagi* Sword) was taken out from its tail and was given to the Emperor's family as one of the three sacred treasures. Later, the sword was dedicated to the *Atsuta-jingu* Shrine in *Owari*(*Aichi* Prefecture). *Omiwa* Shrine whose ghost is Mt. *Miwa* that had strong ties with the Emperor's family also enshrines *Omononushi-no-Kami*, who was originally a snake.

今では姿を現しただけで悲鳴をあげられ、石を投げつけられ、すっかり嫌われものとなったヘビ。しかし、縄文時代には、ヘビを飾りにした土器がありました。弥生時代の銅鐸にはヘビが描かれているものもあります。どうも昔の人々は現代人とは違うヘビへの感情があったようです。

日本は、稲作農業の伝来により、弥生時代に農耕社会になったのですが、農耕に欠かせないものが水です。ヘビは水辺などの湿地を好み、その姿からも、水神の龍の子、あるいは龍の使者としてとらえられ、「ミズチ」として信仰の対象になったのです。

ですから、神話の世界には多くのヘビが登場します。スサノオノミコトが出雲で退治したヤマタノオロチ(八岐大蛇)。これは農業を妨害する悪神として登場しますが、その尾から出たのがクサナギノツルギ(草薙の剣)で、三種の神器として天皇家に受け継がれ、そののち農耕を守護する尾張(愛知県)の熱田神宮に納められました。天皇家とゆかりの深い三輪山をご神体とする大神神社、ここでは大物主神を祭っていますが、大物主神もヘビでした。

Chapter 2
The Middle Ages

The Time of Samurai, the Time of Wars

第2章　中世
武士の時代、争乱の時代

19. The Growth of Samurai and the Local Revolts

① When regency government were at their best, thanes and powerful peasants in local areas revolted against *Koku-shi* or struggled with each other for land. ② Among them, people who specialized in military arts were called *Bushi* (samurai), and they came into power.

③ In the middle of the 10th century, *Taira-no-Masakado* raised a revolt in *Kanto* area and *Fujiwara-no-Sumitomo* did the same thing in the *Seto* inland sea. ④ But the Court broke them down by using other samurai. ⑤ Samurai formed *Bushi-dan*. ⑥ Among the *Bushi-dan*, the *Gen-ji* family and the *Hei-shi* family gained strength.

⑦ In the latter half of the 11th century, in *Tohoku*, battles of thanes arose twice: *Zen-9nen-no-eki* and *Go-3nen-no-eki*. ⑧ But *Minamoto-no-Yoshiie* broke them down with samurai in *Kanto,* so the *Gen-ji* family got power in eastern Japan.

⁹ After that, in *Tohoku*, the *Oshu-Fujiwara* family gained strength. ¹⁰ They established the *Amida* hall, *Chuson-ji-Konjiki-do* in *Hiraizumi*.

---

19. 武士の成長と地方の反乱

①摂関政治が盛んなころ、地方では豪族や有力な農民が国司に対抗したり、土地をめぐって互いに争うようになりました。②なかでも武芸を専門にする者は**武士**と呼ばれ、力をのばしました。
③10世紀の中ごろ、関東では**平将門**が、瀬戸内海では**藤原純友**が反乱を起こしました。④しかし、朝廷は武士の力によって反乱をおさえました。⑤武士は、**武士団**を形成しました。⑥武士団のなかでは、**源氏**と**平氏**の勢力が強くなりました。
⑦11世紀後半、東北地方で、**前九年の役**、**後三年の役**と呼ばれる二度の豪族の争いが起こりました。⑧しかし、**源義家**が関東の武士を率いてこれをしずめ、源氏は東日本で大きな勢力をもちました。⑨その後東北地方では、**奥州藤原氏**が勢力を強めました。⑩そして**平泉**(岩手県)に**中尊寺金色堂**を建てました。

20. The Insei (The Rule by the Cloistered Emperors)

①In the middle of the 11th century, *Gosanjo* became the Emperor. ②He carried out the government with the Emperor at its center using middle and low grade nobles. ③He also seized illegal *Sho-en* and checked farmlands in all over the country to tell *Sho-en* from *Ko-ryo* and to secure stable tax revenue.

④Emperor *Shirakawa* went on to carry out the government with the Emperor at its center. ⑤He remained at the helm as a *Joko* (cloistered Emperor), after he gave up his seat to the next boy Emperor. ⑥As the court of *Joko* was called *In*, this government is called *Insei*.

⑦Political power was transferred from the *Fujiwara* family to *In*. ⑧By quarrels for *Sho-en*, armed priests went to the Court and *In*. ⑨*In* and the nobles hired the samurai of the *Gen-ji* family and the *Hei-shi* family to

第2章 中世 ●武士の時代、争乱の時代

protect themselves against the armed priests.
守る
⑩ Because of this, samurai began to get power in the
　　　　　　　　　　　　　　力をつけつつあった
central government. ⑪ *Toba-joko* and *Goshirakawa-*
　　　　　　　　　　　　　鳥羽上皇　　　　　　後白河上皇
joko continued carrying out *Insei*. ⑫ When *Insei* was at
　　　　　　　　　　　　　　　　　　　　　　　　　全盛であった
its best, the *Fujiwara* family were losing their power.
　　　　　　　　　　　　　　　　力を失いつつあった

---

20. 院政

①11世紀中ごろ、後三条天皇が即位しました。②後三条天皇は、中・下級貴族を使って、天皇中心の政治を行ないました。③また、不法な荘園を整理し、全国の耕地を調べて荘園と公領を確定し、安定した税の確保を目指しました。

④次に即位した白河天皇も、天皇中心の政治を進めました。⑤そして、幼少の天皇に位を譲ったのちも、上皇となって政治の実権を握りました。⑥上皇の御所を院と呼んだので、この政治を院政といいます。

⑦政治の実権は藤原氏から院へ移りました。⑧一方、荘園の争いなどがもとで、僧兵が朝廷や院におしかけるようになりました。⑨院や貴族は僧兵に対抗するため源氏や平氏などの武士を雇いました。⑩これは、武士が中央の政治で力をもつきっかけとなりました。⑪鳥羽上皇、後白河上皇も引き続き院政を行ないました。⑫院政が全盛をむかえるとともに、藤原氏の勢いは衰えていきました。

21. The Hei-shi Administration

①When the samurai began to get power in the central government, *Sutoku-joko* fought with his younger brother, Emperor *Goshirakawa*. ②It brought about *Hogen* Disturbance in 1156. ③This war ended in victory for the Emperor's side but *Minamoto-no-Yoshitomo* was not satisfied with the reward after the war and *Heiji* Disturbance broke out. ④*Yoshitomo* was defeated by *Taira-no-Kiyomori* and *Yoritomo* was exiled to *Izu*.

⑤On the other hand, *Taira-no-Kiyomori* became *Daijo-daijin* (grand minister of state) and he was the first samurai who was at the helm of the government.

⑥*Kiyomori* arranged for his daughter to marry the Emperor and her son became the new Emperor. ⑦In the meantime, he traded with Sung.

⑧The *Hei-shi* family were at the height of their

prosperity but invited ill feelings from *In* and the
nobles. ⑨The samurai who were unhappy with *Hei-shi*'s domination rose in arms. ⑩*Minamoto-no-Yoshitsune* chased the *Hei-shi* family west until he destroyed them in *Dan-no-ura* in 1185.

21. 平氏の政権

①武士が中央で勢力をのばしはじめたころ、朝廷では兄の崇徳上皇と弟の後白河天皇が対立していました。②1156年には**保元の乱**が起きました。③この乱は、天皇側の勝利に終わりましたが、乱後の恩賞に不満をもった源義朝は兵を挙げ、**平治の乱**が起こりました。④源義朝は平清盛に敗れ、このとき頼朝は伊豆（静岡県）に流されました。

⑤一方、平清盛は、**太政大臣**となり、武士としてはじめて政治の実権を握りました。⑥清盛は、娘を天皇の后にし、生まれた子を天皇に立てました。⑦また、宋との貿易を行ないました。

⑧栄華をほこった平氏でしたが、院や貴族の反感を招くことになりました。⑨そのうちに、平氏の支配に不満をもつ諸国の武士が兵を挙げました。⑩**源義経**は、平氏を追って西に進み、1185年、ついに**壇ノ浦**（山口県）で平氏を滅ぼしました。

22. The Taira-Minamoto War （源平の合戦）

My daughter is the Empress. I'm the *Daijo-daijin*.
私の娘は天皇の后。私は太政大臣だ。

平清盛

木曽では源 義仲

伊豆では源頼朝

平氏一門は高位高官を独占し、強大な権力をほこっていました。

そんな平氏に対する反感がつのり、各地で武士が挙兵しました。

Don't fail to kill *Yoritomo*!
頼朝の首を必ずとれ！

I'm *Yoshitsune*. I fight alongside my brother.
私は源義経だ。兄頼朝とともに戦うぞ。

平清盛が熱病で死去しました。

源頼朝は東国一帯を支配下に置きました。

The *Minamoto* family forced us, the *Hei-shi* family, out of the capital.
我々平氏は都から追い出されました。

源義仲はたちまち京へ攻め上りました。

56

第 2 章 中世●武士の時代、争乱の時代

People in *Kyoto* dislike us ...
京の人々に嫌われてしまった…

Hei-shi, stop!
平氏、待て〜！

一ノ谷
壇ノ浦
屋島

しかし義仲は後白河上皇の命令により、義経らに滅ぼされました。

頼朝は弟義経(よしつね)らに平氏を追討させました。

It's all over for me.
もはやこれまで。

We'll go to the undersea capital.
海の底にも都はございます。

1185年、平氏は壇ノ浦の戦いで敗北し、滅亡しました。
8歳の安徳天皇（清盛の孫）は海に身を投げました。

The *Kamakura* period begins.
鎌倉時代の始まりだ。

The tales of the *Heike* family ...
平家物語〜♪

Poor thing.
かわいそう…

平氏滅亡後、源頼朝は本拠を鎌倉に定め、武家政治を確立しました。

平氏の盛衰は琵琶法師によって語られました。

23. The Kamakura Shogunate

①*Minamoto-no-Yoritomo* established a base at *Kamakura*. ②He entered into master-servant relationships with samurai and made them *Gokenin* (his followers). ③He developed the system of the government by samurai. ④*Yoritomo* placed *Shugo* (provincial constable) in each state and *Jito* (estate steward) in each *Sho-en* or *Ko-ryo*, on the grounds of capturing *Yoshitsune*. ⑤When *Yoshitsune* escaped into the *Oshu-Fujiwara* family, he defeated them. ⑥*Yoritomo* was appointed to *Seii-tai-shogun* (Barbarian Subduing General) and an administration by samurai was born in *Kamakura*. ⑦This is called the *Kamakura* shogunate.

⑧The system of the *Kamakura* shogunate was simple. ⑨It consisted of *Samurai-dokoro* (Board of Retainer), *Man-dokoro* (Administrative Board) and *Monchu-jo* (Board of Inquiry). ⑩Shogun protected *Gokenin*'s

territories and he gave them new ones. ⑪This is called
領土
Go-on. ⑫On the other hand, *Gokenin* gave their loyalty
御恩　　　　　　　　　　　　　～に忠誠を誓った
to shogun, guarded *Kamakura* and *Kyoto* and took part
　　　　警備した　　　　　　　　　　　　　　～に参加した
in war. ⑬This is called *Ho-ko*.
　　　　　　　　　　　奉公

23．鎌倉幕府

①源 頼朝は、鎌倉（神奈川県）を本拠地と定めました。②そして、武士と主従関係を結んで御家人としました。③こうして武士による政治のしくみを整えていきました。④頼朝は、弟の義経を捕らえるという口実で、国ごとに**守護**を、荘園・公領ごとに**地頭**を置きました。⑤義経が奥州藤原氏のもとに逃れると、奥州藤原氏を攻め滅ぼしました。⑥頼朝は征夷大将軍に任じられ、鎌倉に武士の政権が生まれました。⑦これを**鎌倉幕府**といいます。

⑧鎌倉幕府のしくみは簡素なものでした。⑨役所として、**侍所**、**政所**、**問注所**などが置かれました。⑩将軍は御家人の領地を保護し、新しい領地を与えました。⑪これを**御恩**といいます。⑫一方、御家人は将軍に忠誠を誓い、鎌倉や京都を警備し、戦いが起こると参加しました。⑬これを**奉公**といいます。

24. The Shikken Government and Jokyu Disturbance

①After the death of *Minamoto-no-Yoritomo*, his son, *Yoriie*, became shogun but *Yoritomo*'s widow, *Masako*, and her father, *Hojo Tokimasa*, were at the helm of the government. ②Later, *Yoriie* was assassinated and *Yoriie*'s brother, *Sanetomo*, became shogun but he was also assassinated by his nephew, *Kugyo*.

③The *Hojo* family became *Shikken* (Regent) from generation to generation. ④After *Yoritomo*'s death, *Hojo Tokimasa*, *Masako* and her brother, *Hojo Yoshitoki*, carried out the government of the shogunate. ⑤After *Minamoto*'s (*Gen-ji*'s) shoguns became extinct, the *Hojo* family practically took power of the shogunate as a *Shikken*. ⑥This government by the *Hojo* family is called *Shikken* government.

⑦Meanwhile, *Gotoba-joko* in the Court wanted to defeat the *Kamakura* shogunate and come into power again. ⑧In 1221, he rose in arms to kill *Hojo Yoshitoki*. ⑨This is called

第2章 中世●武士の時代、争乱の時代

Jokyu Disturbance. ⑩But he was defeated by the
承久の乱
shogunate and exiled to *Oki*.
　　　　　　　～へ追放された　隠岐
⑪After *Jokyu* Disturbance, the shogunate placed its

agencies, *Rokuhara-tandai*, in *Kyoto* to keep watch on
機関　　六波羅探題　　　　　　　　　　　　　～を監視する
the Court. ⑫This let the shogunate more powerful.

24．執権政治と承久の乱

①源 頼朝が死ぬと、頼朝の子頼家が将軍となりましたが、政治の中心は頼朝の妻政子とその父北条時政が握りました。②やがて頼家は暗殺され、その後、頼家の弟実朝が将軍となりましたが、おいの公暁に暗殺されました。

③北条氏は代々、将軍の補佐役である執権の地位につきました。④頼朝の死後は北条時政や政子の弟北条義時らが、政子とともに幕府の政治を動かしていきました。⑤源氏の将軍が絶えた後、幕府の権力は執権の職にある北条氏が握る形となりました。⑥このような北条氏による政治を、執権政治といいます。

⑦朝廷では後鳥羽上皇が、鎌倉幕府を倒し、権力を朝廷にもどすことをめざして兵を整えつつありました。⑧そして1221年、北条義時追討の命令を出して挙兵しました。⑨これを承久の乱といいます。⑩しかし、幕府の大軍に敗れ、上皇は隠岐（島根県）に流されました。

⑪承久の乱の後、幕府は朝廷の監視のために、京都に六波羅探題を置きました。⑫これにより、幕府の支配力は西におよび、一段と強くなりました。

25. The Goseibai-shikimoku and the Life of Samurai

①After *Jokyu* Disturbance, *Shikken Hojo Yasutoki* (泰時) sought political stability (政治の安定を求める) through negotiations of (~の話し合いによって) *Gokenin*. ②He also set up *Hyojoshu* (設ける) (Council of State) (評定衆). ③The customs (慣習) of samurai society (武家社会) were put in writing (文書にまとめられる) by *Yasutoki* in 1232 (*Goseibai-shikimoku*) (御成敗式目). ④It was the first law samurai made.

⑤Samurai's houses were simple (簡素な) and practical (実用的な), and they made walls (塀) and moats (堀) around them in preparation for (~に備えて) battles. ⑥They ruled their villages as *Shokan* (荘官) (Sho-en manager) or *Jito* (地頭) and collected tributes (年貢を取り立てた). ⑦They made *Genin* (下人) and peasants cultivate fields around their houses.

⑧It was important for samurai to develop military arts (武芸をみがくこと). ⑨Among military arts, three games were especially well-practiced: *Kasagake* (笠懸) (practical (実戦上の) horseback riding archery), *Inuoumono* (犬追物) (dog hunting) and *Yabusame* (流鏑馬)

62

(ritual horseback riding archery).
儀式上の

⑩Giving their loyalty to their masters by working on
　　主人へ忠誠を誓うこと　　　　　　　　　　　　　～にはげむ
military arts was a morally right behavior for samurai
　　　　　　　　　　道徳的に正しい行ない
and it was called *Mononofu-no-michi* or *Kyu-ba-no-*
　　　　　　　　　　もののふの道　　　　　　弓馬の道
michi.

---

25. 御成敗式目と武士の生活

①承久の乱の後、執権**北条泰時**は、有力な御家人の話し合いによって政治の安定をはかりました。②そして、評議を行う役所として、**評定衆**を置きました。③また泰時は、1232年、武家社会の慣習を文書にまとめ、**御成敗式目（貞永式目）**を制定しました。④御成敗式目は、武士のつくった最初の法律でした。

⑤武士の住まいは簡素で実用的なもので、戦いに備えてまわりに**塀**や**堀**をめぐらせていました。⑥武士は荘官や地頭として村を支配し、**年貢**を取り立てました。⑦また館の周辺の田畑を下人や農民に耕作させていました。

⑧また武士は、武芸をみがくことが第一とされていました。⑨武芸の中では、**笠懸・犬追物・流鏑馬**の3つの弓技が盛んに行なわれていました。⑩このように武芸にはげみ、主人への忠誠を誓うことは、武士の守るべき道徳とされ、「**もののふの道**」や「**弓馬の道**」などと呼ばれました。

26. The Dual Control and the Life of Peasants

①Even after the government by the shogunate began, the Court and nobles went on ruling the *Sho-en* as *Sho-en-Ryoshu*. ②Peasants were under dual control of *Kuge* (court noble) and *Buke* (samurai family).
③The Court was in Kyoto and Kyoto flourished as the center of the government by *Kuge*. ④The shogunate was in *Kamakura* and *Kamakura* flourished as the center of the government by *Buke*.

⑤Peasants paid tributes to *Sho-en-Ryoshu* but samurai often ruled land and peasants as *Jito*, so there were quarrels between *Sho-en-Ryoshu* and *Jito*. ⑥Therefore, *Sho-en-Ryoshu* gave half of their *Sho-en* to *Jito*(*Shitaji-chubun*) or let *Jito* control *Sho-en* provided that *Jito* paid a certain rate of tributes (*Jito-uke*).

⑦Farm technique was improved. ⑧Cultivation by cows

and horses spread and peasants double-cropped in
western Japan. ⁹Markets to exchange goods were held
regularly.

広まる / 二毛作をした / 市

26．二重の支配と農民の生活

①幕府による政治が始まっても、朝廷や貴族は荘園領主として引き続き全国の荘園を支配していました。②そのため、農民は、**公家**(くげ)と**武家**(ぶけ)による二重の支配を受けていました。

③朝廷がある京都は公家の政治の中心地として栄えました。

④また、幕府がある**鎌倉**は武家の政治の中心地として栄えました。

⑤農民は年貢を荘園領主に納めていましたが、武士が地頭となって土地や農民を支配することが多くなり、荘園領主と地頭との間でしばしば争いが起こりました。⑥そのため荘園領主は、荘園の土地を半分地頭に分けたり(**下地中分**(したじちゅうぶん))、一定の年貢を納めさせる条件をつけて荘園の管理をいっさい地頭に任せたり(**地頭請**(じとううけ))しました。

⑦鎌倉時代は農業技術が高まった時代でもありました。⑧**牛馬**(ぎゅうば)を使った耕作が広まり、西日本では**二毛作**(にもうさく)も行なわれるようになりました。⑨商品をやりとりするための**市**(いち)も定期的に開かれました。

27. The Mongol Invasion（元の襲来）

モンゴル帝国のフビライは国号を元として、北京を都にしました。

フビライは日本を服属させようと何度も使者を送りました。

鎌倉幕府の執権北条時宗は元の使者を無視し続けました。

1274年、ついに元が北九州に襲来しました。

第2章　中世●武士の時代、争乱の時代

> I'm done for.
> やられた～。

幕府軍は元の集団戦法や火薬に苦しめられました。

> The enemy's ships have gone!
> 敵の船がいなくなったぞ！

ところが暴風雨が起こり、元軍は引き揚げました。

> For God's sake ...
> ひどい……

フビライは再び使者を送りましたが、幕府は処刑してしまいました。

> We cannot go ashore because of the barricade.
> 海岸に石塁があって上陸できない。

1281年、元は再び来襲しました。

> A divine wind has blown.
> 神風が吹いたぞ～！

再び暴風雨が起こり、元軍は大損害を受けました。

> There is no reward, huh.
> ほうびがないね。
>
> We have become badly off.
> 生活が苦しくなったよ。

御家人 Gokenin

十分な恩賞がもらえなかった御家人の生活は苦しくなりました。

28. Kamakura Culture

①Samurai and people spent every day in uncertainty because of wars and famines, so they turned to new Buddhism sects called *Kamakura-shin-bukkyo*. ②The teaching of them was so easy to understand that they became popular among them.

③*Honen* insisted that people should faithfully obey the teaching of *Jodo-shinko* and founded *Jodo-shu*. ④His disciple, *Shinran*, founded *Jodo-shin-shu*. ⑤*Nichiren* founded *Nichiren-shu*. ⑥*Ippen* founded *Ji-shu* and spread a dance prayer. ⑦*Zen-shu* was introduced from Sung. ⑧It was suited for the spirit of samurai. ⑨*Eisai* founded *Rinzai-shu* and *Dogen* founded *Soto-shu*.

⑩In the *Kamakura* period, simple and powerful culture developed. ⑪The life of samurai and war were described in *The Tales of the Heike* and it was passed by word of mouth of *Biwa* minstrel. ⑫Excellent essays

were written: _The Ten Foot Square Hut_ by _Kamo-no-Chomei_ 『方丈記』 鴨長明
and _Essays in Idleness_ by _Yoshida Kenko_. 『徒然草』 吉田兼好
⑬_Fujiwara-no-Teika_ and others edited _New Collection of Ancient and Modern_. 藤原定家 『新古今和歌集』
⑭_Kongo-rikishi-zo_ was graved by _Unkei_ and _Kaikei_. 金剛力士像 彫られた 運慶 快慶

28. 鎌倉文化

①戦乱やききんなどの災害が続き、不安な日々を送ってきた武士や庶民は、鎌倉新仏教とよばれる新しい仏教に救いを求めるようになりました。②いずれの教えもわかりやすかったことから、武士や庶民に広まっていきました。

③法然は、浄土信仰の教えを徹底することを主張し、浄土宗を開きました。④その弟子の親鸞は、浄土真宗(一向宗)を開きました。⑤日蓮は日蓮宗(法華宗)を開きました。⑥一遍は時宗を開き、踊念仏を広めました。⑦宋からは禅宗が伝わりました。⑧禅宗は武士の気風に合っていました。⑨栄西は臨済宗を、道元は曹洞宗を開きました。

⑩鎌倉時代には、素朴で力強い文化が発達しました。⑪武士の生活や戦乱を描いた『平家物語』は、琵琶法師によって語り伝えられました。⑫鴨長明の『方丈記』、吉田兼好の『徒然草』などのすぐれた随筆も書かれました。⑬歌集では、藤原定家らにより『新古今和歌集』が編集されました。⑭彫刻では、運慶・快慶による金剛力士像が知られています。

29. The New Government of Kemmu

① The *Kamakura* shogunate passed through the crisis of the Mongol invasions but *Gokenin*, who were not adequately rewarded, were unhappy with the shogunate.

② Emperor *Godaigo* took advantage of this opportunity and rose in arms to defeat the shogunate and return to the government with the Emperor at its center.

③ Samurai collected by Emperor *Godaigo* were *Kusunoki Masashige* and others, who were unhappy with the government by the shogunate. ④ The shogunate placed a great army in *Kyoto* and tried to break down the revolt. ⑤ Nevertheless, estrangement of powerful *Gokenin*, *Ashikaga Takauji*, changed the whole picture. ⑥ *Ashikaga Takauji* took control of *Rokuhara-tandai* in 1333 and *Nitta Yoshisada* captured *Kamakura*. ⑦ At last, the *Kamakura*

shogunate was ruined.
　　　　　　　　滅亡した
⁸The government of Emperor *Godaigo* is called *Kemmu-no-shinsei* (New Government of *Kemmu*).
建武の新政
⁹Samurai, however, were disappointed with his
　　　　　　　　　　～に失望した
government which made much of *Kuge*, and it lasted
　　　　　　　～を重視した
only two years.

---

29. 建武の新政

①鎌倉幕府は、元寇の危機を切り抜けましたが、十分な恩賞をもらえなかった御家人は幕府への不満を高めました。
②このタイミングを利用して、**後醍醐天皇**は、幕府を倒して天皇中心の政治を復活させようと兵を挙げました。③後醍醐天皇が動員したのは、**楠木正成**など幕府の政治に不満をもつ武士でした。④幕府は、大軍を京都に派遣して鎮圧をはかりました。
⑤しかし、それでも有力御家人の**足利尊氏**が離反すると状況は大きく変わりました。⑥1333年には足利尊氏が六波羅探題を陥落させ、**新田義貞**が鎌倉を攻略しました。⑦そして、ついに鎌倉幕府は滅亡しました。
⑧後醍醐天皇の政治を、**建武の新政**と呼びます。⑨しかし、公家重視の政治は武士の失望をまねき、新政は2年ほどで失敗に終わりました。

30. The Disturbance of the Northern and Southern Court

①The Emperor tried to unify *Kuge* and *Buke* under him by *Kemmu-no-shinsei* but expectation gave way to disappointment. ②Good rewards to *Kuge* disappointed samurai. ③Further, samurai in each state were displeased with the Emperor's plan to build a vast palace because of the great expense they would have to pay for it.

④With a backdrop of this discontent of samurai, *Ashikaga Takauji* stood up to get back the government by samurai. ⑤*Ashikaga Takauji* held *Kyoto* in 1336 and made *Komyo* the Emperor. ⑥Emperor *Komyo* was a legitimate descendant of *Jimyoin* and had a conflict with Emperor *Godaigo*, who was a legitimate descendant of *Daikakuji*. ⑦Emperor *Godaigo* escaped to *Yoshino* and the Courts were placed both in *Kyoto* and in *Yoshino*. ⑧The one in *Kyoto* was called *Hoku-cho* (the northern Court) and the other in *Yoshino* was called *Nan-cho* (the southern Court).[9] This was the beginning of the *Nanboku-cho* disturbance (the Disturbance of the Northern and Southern Court). [10] This disturbance lasted about 60 years.

30. 南北朝の動乱

[1]天皇のもとに公家と武家を統合しようとした建武の新政でしたが、その期待はまもなく失望に変わりました。[2]公家重視の恩賞は武士の期待を裏切りました。[3]そのうえ大規模な宮殿の造営計画は、費用を負担する諸国の武士の不満を増大させるものとなったのです。

[4]こうした武士の不満を背景に、武家政治の再興を目指して立ち上がったのが足利尊氏です。[5]1336年、京都を制圧した足利尊氏は、光明天皇を擁立しました。[6]持明院統の光明天皇は、大覚寺統の後醍醐天皇と対立しました。[7]後醍醐天皇は吉野へ脱出し、京都と吉野に朝廷が並立することになりました。[8]京都の朝廷を北朝、吉野の朝廷を南朝といいます。[9]これが南北朝の動乱の始まりです。[10]この動乱は、約60年間続きました。

31. The Muromachi Shogunate

①*Ashikaga Takauji* was appointed as *Seii-tai-shogun* (Barbarian Subduing General) by *Hoku-cho* (the northern Court) in 1338. ②The shogunate of the *Ashikaga* family is called the *Muromachi* shogunate.

③The system of the *Muromachi* shogunate was largely like that of the *Kamakura* shogunate but shogun's assistant was named *Kanrei*. ④Powerful *Shugo-Daimyo* (official feudal lord) who were in the *Ashikaga* family were appointed as *Kanrei*: *Hosokawa*, *Shiba* and *Hatakeyama*. ⑤*Samurai-dokoro* was also an important agency. ⑥The head of *Samurai-dokoro* was called *Shoshi* and four families took up the post by rotation: *Akamatsu*, *Isshiki*, *Yamana* and *Kyogoku*. ⑦They were other powerful *Shugo-Daimyo*.

⑧One of the characteristics of the *Muromachi* shogunate was that *Shugo* had strong power. ⑨During

the *Nanboku-cho* disturbance, *Shugo* got the power to collect a half of tributes as <u>*Hyoro-mai*</u> (rice for troops) by the system of <u>*Hanzeirei*</u> and ruled over their 兵糧米 半済令
<u>territories</u> powerfully. ⑩They <u>entered into master-</u> 領地 ～と主従関係を結んだ
servant relationships with <u>domestic</u> *Jito* and they grew 国内の
into *Shugo-Daimyo*.

---

31. 室町幕府

①1338年、足利尊氏は北朝から征夷大将軍に任じられました。②足利氏の幕府を室町幕府と呼びます。

③室町幕府のしくみは、ほぼ鎌倉幕府にならったものですが、将軍の補佐役は管領といいます。④管領には細川・斯波・畠山という足利氏一門の有力守護大名がつきました。⑤また室町幕府では、侍所も重要な機関でした。⑥侍所の長官は所司と呼ばれ、赤松・一色・山名・京極の4氏が交代で就任しました。⑦彼らもまた有力な守護大名でした。

⑧室町幕府の特色の1つは、守護の力が強かったことです。⑨南北朝の動乱に際し、半済令により兵糧米として年貢の半分を徴収する権限を得た守護は、領地支配を強めていきました。⑩そして国内の地頭と主従関係を結び、守護大名へと成長しました。

32. The Kango Trade

①During the *Nanboku-cho* disturbance in Japan, Japanese pirates called *Wako* infested East Asia. ②Han people's Ming was established in place of Mongol people's Yuan in China in 1368. ③Ming frequently required Japan to crack down on *Wako*. ④*Ashikaga Yoshimitsu* prohibited the piracy at the request of Ming and started to trade with Ming officially. ⑤Trade with Ming was called *Kango* trade because tally sticks (*Kango*) were used to tell trading vessels from pirate ships. ⑥*Kango* trade brought profit to the *Muromachi* shogunate but the real power of the trade gradually transferred to the *Ouchi* family, who dealt with *Hakata* merchants, and the *Hosokawa* family, who dealt with *Sakai* merchants. ⑦The main exported goods of Japan in *Kango* trade were sulfur, swords and fans, and the main imported ones were bronze coins and raw silk.

⁸On the Korean Peninsula, Goryeo was ruined and
　　　　　　　　　　　　　　　高麗
Korea was established. ⁹They developed Hangul to
朝鮮国　　　　　　　　　　　　　　　　　ハングル文字
write down the Korean language and they began to
書き表す
trade with Japan.

32. 勘合貿易

①日本国内で南北朝の動乱が続いていたころ、東アジアでは、**倭寇**と呼ばれる日本人の海賊集団が猛威をふるっていました。②中国では1368年、モンゴル民族の元に代わり、漢民族の**明**が建てられました。③明は、日本に対したびたび倭寇の取り締まりを求めてきました。④**足利義満**はこれに応じ、倭寇の活動を禁じるとともに、明と正式な貿易を開始しました。⑤明との貿易は、貿易船と海賊船とを区別するため、**勘合**という合札が用いられたので、**勘合貿易**と呼ばれました。⑥勘合貿易は、室町幕府にばく大な利益をもたらしましたが、しだいにその実権は博多商人と結んだ**大内氏**や、堺商人と結んだ**細川氏**に移っていきました。⑦勘合貿易における日本の主な輸出品は硫黄、刀剣、扇、主な輸入品は銅銭、生糸でした。
⑧朝鮮半島では高麗が滅び、かわって**朝鮮国**が建てられました。
⑨朝鮮語を書き表す**ハングル**という文字がつくられ、日本との貿易も開始されました。

33. The Development of Industry and Economy

①In the *Muromachi* period, society was stabilized and industry developed in various parts of the country because of the trade with China and Korea.

②As for agriculture, double cropping spread to all over the country. ③People got a better harvest by using cows and horses. ④Cultivation of commercial crops became popular.

⑤In the handicraft industry, local specialties such as silk fabric in *Nishijin* and earthenware in *Seto* were produced in large quantities. ⑥Forge and foundry industry also flourished. ⑦In commerce, markets were held all over the country more often than before.

⑧Handicraftsmen and merchants formed a trading association called *Za*. ⑨*Za* monopolized the market under the care of nobles and temples.

⑩The development of commerce and industry brought

that of finance and circulation. ⑪Pawnshops called *Doso* appeared. ⑫Water transport was developed in the *Seto* inland sea and Lake *Biwa*. ⑬Carriers and warehousers called *Toiya* did business at harbors. ⑭Moreover, carriers called *Bashaku* flourished on land.

33．産業と経済の発達

①室町時代は社会がやや安定し、中国や朝鮮との貿易により、各地で産業が発達しました。
②農業では、二毛作が各地に広まりました。③耕作に牛や馬を利用して、収穫が増えました。④また商品作物の栽培が盛んになりました。
⑤手工業では西陣（京都）の絹織物、瀬戸の陶器など各地で特産物の生産が進みました。⑥鍛冶・鋳物業なども盛んになりました。⑦商業では、市が各地で開かれ、開催日数も増えました。
⑧手工業者や商人は、座と呼ばれる同業者の組合をつくっていました。⑨座は貴族や寺社の保護のもとに営業を独占していました。
⑩商工業の発達は、金融や流通の発達をもたらしました。⑪土倉と呼ばれる質屋が現れました。⑫瀬戸内海や琵琶湖などの水上交通が発達しました。⑬港では問屋と呼ばれる運送業・倉庫業者が活動しました。⑭また、馬借と呼ばれる陸上の運送業者も活躍しました。

34. The Formation of the Soson

① Agriculture developed and the produce which remained in the peasants' hands increased, so villagers came to make good livings. ② Some powerful peasants became *Ji-zamurai* (local samurai).

③ These new samurai, *Kokujin* (powerful local samurai) and powerful peasants formed villages with the people around them. ④ In some villages, the people fenced and moated their villages in preparation for battle. ⑤ *Yoriai*, which consisted mainly of powerful peasants, ran their village. ⑥ Some villages laid down rules and punished violators. ⑦ *Ichimishinsui* (the ceremony of drinking water with ash of written oath in it) was performed for the village solidarity. ⑧ These self-governing councils are called *So*, and villages run by the bond of *So* are called *Soson*.

⑨ Peasants bonded by *So* became stronger to oppose

Shoen-Ryoshu or *Shugo-Daimyo*. ⑩Some negotiated [交渉した] as a group [集団で] with them about reduction of tributes [年貢を減らすことについて]. ⑪Others fired [やめさせた] *Sho-kan* who had ruthlessly [冷酷に] collected [取り立てた] tributes and paid tributes directly.

---

34. 惣村の形成

①農業が発達すると農民の手元に残る生産物が増え、村の生活は豊かになりました。②有力な農民の中には新たに武士となって、**地侍**となる者も現れました。

③こうした新しい武士や**国人**、有力な農民を中心にして村が生まれました。④村によっては、戦乱にそなえて村のまわりに柵や堀をめぐらす者もいました。

⑤村の運営は、有力な農民を主なメンバーとする**寄合**によって行なわれました。⑥また、村の掟を定め、違反者をきびしく罰するところもありました。⑦村人の団結のために**一味神水**も行なわれました。⑧こうした自治組織を**惣**、惣による結合をもとに運営される村落を**惣村**といいます。

⑨惣に結合した農民は、荘園領主や守護大名に対抗する力を強めていきました。⑩なかには集団で年貢を減らすように交渉した農民もいました。⑪あるいは無理な取り立てをする**荘官**をやめさせて、惣の責任で年貢を納めるようにした者もいました。

35. The Self-governing by the Ikki

①The *Muromachi* period was when violent means [実力行動] called *Ikki* [一揆] by peasants and *Ji-zamurai* [地侍] often broke out. ②*Do-ikki* [土一揆], *Kuni-ikki* [国一揆] and *Ikko-ikki* [一向一揆] are very famous. ③*Do-ikki* was the violent means by peasants called *Do-min* [土民], and they demanded to [～するように要求した] wipe all of their debts [帳消しにする] [借金] away and to reduce tributes. ④A typical [代表的な] *Do-ikki* was *Shocho-no-do-ikki* [正長の土一揆] in 1428. ⑤*Bashaku* [馬借] (carrier by horses) in *Omi* [近江] and peasants in the suburbs of [～の近郊] *Kyoto* stood up to press the shogunate [幕府に対して～を要求する] to issue the decree [法令を発布すること], *Tokusei-rei* [徳政令], and tore up [破棄した] their debts by hitting [襲う] liquor stores and *Doso* [土倉].

⑥*Kuni-ikki* [国一揆] was started mainly by *Kokujin*. ⑦A typical *Kuni-ikki* was *Yamashiro-no-kuni-ikki* [山城の国一揆] in 1485. ⑧In southern *Yamashiro*, *Kokujin* and peasants stood up together to purge [追放する] *Shugo-Daimyo* and they achieved [自治を達成した] self-rule for eight years.

⁹Priests who believed in *Jodo-shin-shu* (*Ikko-shu*), *Kokujin* and peasants rose in *Ikko-ikki*. ¹⁰A typical *Ikko-ikki* was *Kaga-no-ikko-ikki* in 1488. ¹¹This broke out in *Kaga* and the *Togashi* family, the *Shugo-Daimyo*, was defeated.

35．一揆による自治

①室町時代は、一揆と呼ばれる農民や地侍の団結と、それをもとにした実力行動が目立った時代でした。②有名な一揆には土一揆、国一揆、一向一揆などがあります。

③土一揆とは土民と呼ばれた農民の実力行動で、借金の帳消しや年貢の減額を求めて起こしました。④土一揆の代表的なものが1428（正長元）年の正長の土一揆です。⑤これは、借金に苦しむ近江（滋賀県）の馬借や、京都近郊の農民が立ち上がり、借金の約束を破棄させる徳政令を幕府に要求し、酒屋や土倉を襲って借金の証文を破り捨てたものです。

⑥国一揆とは、国人を中心とする一揆です。⑦国一揆の代表的なものが1485年の山城の国一揆です。⑧これは、山城（京都府）南部で、国人と農民が一体となって立ち上がり、守護大名を追放して8年間自治を行なったものです。

⑨一向一揆は、親鸞の教えである浄土真宗（一向宗）を信仰する僧侶、国人、農民が団結して起こした一揆です。⑩一向一揆の代表的なものが1488年の加賀の一向一揆です。⑪これは、加賀（石川県）で起こり、守護大名の富樫氏を倒したものです。

36. The Onin War

①The *Muromachi* shogunate was like a coalition government of *Shugo-Daimyo*. ②The assassination of *Ashikaga Yoshinori*, the 6th shogun, and *Ikki* all around the country took the power away from the shogunate. ③The struggle for power among powerful *Daimyo* became serious. ④Among them, the *Hosokawa* family and the *Yamana* family were the two big powers.

⑤The 8th shogun, *Ashikaga Yoshimasa*, was not interested in the government and his wife, *Hino Tomiko*, was at the helm of the government. ⑥*Yoshimasa* wanted his brother, *Yoshimi*, to be the next shogun.

⑦But *Tomiko* gave birth to a baby boy, *Yoshihisa*, and the next shogun came into question. ⑧It divided the shogunate into two groups.

⑨At last, war broke out in *Kyoto* in 1467. ⑩Some

Shugo-Daimyo were on *Hosokawa*'s side (East Army) and others were on *Yamana*'s side (West Army). ⑪ It lasted eleven years but ended in a draw. ⑫ This war is called the *Onin* war.

東軍 / 西軍 / 続いた / 引き分けに終わった / 応仁の乱

---

36. 応仁の乱

①室町幕府は、守護大名の連立政権のような性格をもっていました。②6代将軍足利義教が暗殺されたり、各地に一揆が起こったりして、幕府の力が弱まりました。③すると有力大名の勢力争いが激しくなりました。④なかでも有力な細川氏と山名氏が勢力を二分していました。

⑤8代将軍となった足利義政は、政治に関心を示さず、政治の実権は義政の妻・日野富子にありました。⑥義政は、弟の義視を次の将軍に指名しました。⑦しかし日野富子に義尚が生まれると、後継者問題が起こりました。⑧それは幕府を二分する争いに発展しました。

⑨そして1467年、ついに京都で戦いが起こりました。⑩諸国の守護大名は細川方(東軍)と山名方(西軍)に分かれて戦いました。⑪争いは11年間続きましたが、明確な決着をみないまま終わりました。⑫これを応仁の乱といいます。

37. The Gekokujo and the Warring Lord

①*Gekokujo* means that low rank people require high rank people to do something or the former defeats the latter. ②*Do-ikki* is one example of it. ③After the *Onin War*, the power of the shogun weakened and he could rule only small areas around *Kyoto*. ④Hence, *Shugo-Daimyo* had to rule their territory by themselves. ⑤Some powerless *Shugo-Daimyo* were defeated by their own servants. ⑥People who had power to rule *Ji-zamurai* and peasants could be rulers of the territory. ⑦These rulers are called *Sengoku-Daimyo* (warring lord).

⑧*Sengoku-Daimyo* ruled their territory under the policy of increasing wealth and military power. ⑨They accepted *Ji-zamurai* as servants to form an army and ruled the land and people to collect tributes. ⑩*Takeda Shingen* in *Kai* extended farmland by flood prevention works and opened mines. ⑪Some *Sengoku-Daimyo*

enacted the ordinance(domestic law): the *Imagawa*
制定した　　　条例　　　領内だけの法律　　　今川家の
family's the *Imagawa-kana-mokuroku* or the *Takeda*
　　　　　『今川仮名目録』　　　　　　　　武田家の
family's *Shingen-kaho*.
　　　『信玄家法』

37. 下剋上と戦国大名

①下の位の者が上の位の者に対して強く要求したり、上の位の者を倒したりすることを下剋上といいます。②土一揆はその一例です。③応仁の乱後、将軍の権威が衰えると、将軍は京都を中心とするわずかな地方を支配するだけとなりました。④それゆえ守護大名は自らの力で領国を支配しなければなりませんでした。⑤そして力の劣った守護大名は、実力をたくわえた家来にその地位を奪われていきました。⑥地侍や農民を治める力をもった者が、領国の支配者となり得ました。⑦こうして生まれた領国の支配者を**戦国大名**といいます。

⑧戦国大名は、**富国強兵**を目指して領国を支配しました。⑨戦国大名は、地侍を家臣に組み入れて強力な軍事組織をつくり上げ、土地と人民を支配して年貢の徴収をはかりました。⑩**甲斐**(山梨県)の**武田信玄**のように治水工事によって耕地を増やすとともに、鉱山の開発を積極的に行なう者もいました。⑪今川氏の『**今川仮名目録**』、武田氏の『**信玄家法**』のように**分国法**という領内だけに適用される法律をつくる戦国大名もいました。

38. The Development of the Cities and the Town People

①Industry and economy developed and cities were built all over the country. ②Castle towns developed around the castles of *Sengoku-Daimyo*. ③They made powerful servants live near their castles and gathered merchants and industrialists. ④Castle towns became the center of politics, economy and culture.

⑤On the other hand, some cities were self-governed by powerful merchants and industrialists such as *Sakai* and *Hakata*, which flourished by the trade with Ming. ⑥Believers, merchants and industrialists got together in the temples of *Ikko-shu*. ⑦Such in-temple towns were also self-governed.

⑧*Kyoto* was self-governed by rich merchants and industrialists called town people. ⑨They held again the *Gion-matsuri* Festival after a long interval of the *Onin* War. ⑩Meanwhile, *Sakai* was self-governed during the

disturbance of war and kept peace. ⑪It was reported to
戦争の動乱　　　　　　　　　　平和を保った
Europe through *Yasokaishi-nihon-tsushin*.
　　　　　　　　　　　　　　　『耶蘇会士日本通信』

38．都市の発展と町衆

①産業や経済の発達に伴って各地に都市が発達しました。②特に戦国大名の居城を中心に**城下町**（じょうかまち）が発達しました。③戦国大名は有力な家臣を城下に住まわせて、商工業者を呼び集めました。④そのため城下町は領内の政治・経済・文化の中心地となりました。

⑤一方、明との貿易で栄えた**堺**（さかい）や**博多**（はかた）など、有力な商工業者による自治が行なわれた都市もありました。⑥**一向宗**（いっこうしゅう）の寺院を中心に信者や商工業者が集まったところもありました。⑦そうした**寺内町**（じないまち）も自治的な都市でした。

⑧京都では**町衆**（まちしゅう）と呼ばれる裕福な商工業者による自治が行なわれていました。⑨**応仁の乱**（おうにん）によってとだえていた**祇園祭**（ぎおんまつり）を復興させたのも町衆の力です。⑩堺は各地で戦国の動乱が続くなかも自治が進められ、平和が保たれていました。⑪このことは、『**耶蘇会士日本通信**』（やそ）によって、ヨーロッパにも伝えられています。

39. Muromachi Culture

① In the *Muromachi* period, shogun and powerful *Shugo-Daimyo* willingly absorbed *Kuge*'s culture, so *Buke*'s culture and *Kuge*'s culture were united.
② *Ashikaga Yoshimitsu* established *Kinkaku-ji* villa in *Kitayama* and the culture at that time is called *Kitayama* culture. ③ Around that time, *Kan-ami* and *Ze-ami* perfected *no* play.
④ *Ashikaga Yoshimasa* established *Ginkaku-ji* villa in *Higashiyama* and the culture at that time is called *Higashiyama* culture. ⑤ The architectural style, *Shoin-zukuri*, accepted the style of the temples, *Zenshu-jiin*, and even now some houses are built in this style with the garden of dry garden style. ⑥ Tea ceremony and *ikebana* (flower arrangement) were also popular.
⑦ *Sesshu* developed his skill of sumi-e in Ming and drew Japanese scenery after coming back to Japan.

⁸The verse linking, *Renga*, became popular among samurai and the common people in place of *Waka* (31-syllable Japanese poem). ⁹Women and children liked stories with drawings called *Otogi-zoshi* based on *The Inch-High Samurai*, *Urashima and the Kingdom Beneath the Sea* and so on.

---

39. 室町文化

①室町時代には、将軍や有力な守護大名が進んで公家の文化を吸収し、武家の文化と公家の文化とがとけ合った文化が生まれました。

②足利義満は、京都の北山に金閣を建てたので、このころ栄えた文化を北山文化といいます。③観阿弥・世阿弥が、能楽を大成させたのもこのころです。

④足利義政は、京都の東山に銀閣を建てたので、このころ栄えた文化を東山文化といいます。⑤書院造は、禅宗寺院の様式が取り入れられたもので、枯山水の庭などとともに現代の住居に息づいています。⑥茶の湯や生け花も流行しました。⑦雪舟は、明に渡って水墨画を深め、帰国後は日本の風景を描きました。

⑧和歌に代わって、連歌が武士や民衆に広まりました。⑨また、『一寸法師』、『浦島太郎』などの話をもとにお伽草子と呼ばれる絵入りの物語がつくられ、女性や子どもに親しまれました。

Dog / イヌ

The Fact Dog-lovers Don't Want to Know
犬好きには知りたくない事実

Dogs have been intimate friends of human beings in both western and eastern countries. We have kept them as guard dogs, gone hunting with them and taken them to the battlefields. They are very useful animals.

Let me tell you two facts you may not believe.

First, people used dogs as targets. From the *Kamakura* period, samurai did various kinds of trainings to develop their military arts. The greatest suffering for dogs was *Inuoumono*(dog hunting). This was a training where dogs were used as targets for samurai on horseback to shoot arrows at. In the *Muromachi* period, there was one large *Inuoumono* that 36 archers shot 150 target dogs, though the arrows had no heads and round tops.

Second, people used to eat dogs. In the period of Emperor *Temmu*, they banned people from eating cows, horses, dogs, monkeys and chickens. There might have been a lot of people that ate them at that time.

人間にとって最も関係の深い動物といえば、洋の東西を問わずイヌでしょう。番犬として、狩猟の供として、時には戦いの場にと、イヌは大活躍です。

さて、「エ一、ウッソー！」というお話をしましょう。

一つは、イヌが標的にされていたこと。鎌倉時代以来、武士たちは普段、自らの武芸をみがくためにさまざまな訓練をしていました。その中で、イヌの受難が「犬追物(いぬおうもの)」です。これはイヌを標的として、武士が馬上から弓矢を放つものです。室町時代には、射手36騎がイヌ150匹を狙うという大規模なものもありました。ただ、イヌを傷つけないように、矢の先端に矢じりは付けず、丸くしていましたが…。

もう一つは、イヌは食用だったということ。古くは天武天皇の時に、「これよりウシ、ウマ、イヌ、サル、ニワトリを食べてはいけません」という禁令が出されました。イヌを食べる人が多かったのでしょう。

Chapter 3
The Modern Ages

The Unification of Japan and the Rise of Common People

第3章 近世
天下統一と庶民の台頭

40. The Arrivals of Guns and Christianity

①A Chinese ship with Portuguese passengers on was caught in a storm and got to the island, *Tanega-shima*, in 1543. ②They were the first Europeans in Japan. ③Guns arrived in Japan at that time. ④*Sengoku-Daimyo* were interested in guns and soon guns started to be made in *Sakai* and other places. ⑤Guns spread quickly and changed the tactics in war. ⑥*Oda Nobunaga* won the *Nagashino* war using guns and defeated *Takeda Katsuyori* in 1575.

⑦Spanish Francis Xavier arrived in *Kagoshima* to teach Christianity in 1549. ⑧He stayed for more than two years in *Yamaguchi*, *Kyoto* and *Bungo-funai*. ⑨Missionaries built schools, hospitals and orphan homes, and they lined up support of people. ⑩At that time, Europeans were called *Nanban-jin* and Christians were called *Kirishitan*. ⑪Some *Daimyo* in *Kyushu*

protected Christianity to trade with Europeans. ⑫Among
保護した
them, some *Daimyo* themselves became Christians and
キリスト教信者
they were called *Kirishitan-Daimyo*.
キリシタン大名

40．鉄砲とキリスト教の伝来

①1543年、**ポルトガル人**を乗せた中国船が、暴風雨にあって**種子島**(鹿児島県)に漂着しました。②日本に来た最初のヨーロッパ人でした。③このとき**鉄砲**が伝えられました。④鉄砲は戦国大名に注目され、短期間のうちに、堺(大阪府)などでつくられるようになりました。⑤鉄砲はたちまち広まり、戦いの際の戦法を変えました。⑥織田信長が鉄砲隊を活用し長篠の戦いに勝利して、武田勝頼を破るのは、1575年のことです。

⑦1549年には、スペイン人の**フランシスコ・ザビエル**がキリスト教を伝えるために、**鹿児島**に上陸しました。⑧ザビエルは、山口、京都、豊後府内(大分市)などで2年余り滞在しました。⑨宣教師は学校や病院・孤児院を建てるなどしたので、民衆の支持を得ていきました。⑩このころ、ヨーロッパ人は**南蛮人**と呼ばれ、キリスト教の信者は**キリシタン**と呼ばれていました。⑪九州の大名の中には、貿易をするために、キリスト教を保護する者もいました。⑫中にはキリスト教の信者になり、**キリシタン大名**と呼ばれる大名も現れました。

41. The Rise of Oda Nobunaga（織田信長の台頭）

> When I was young, I was called an idiot.
> 若いころは「うつけ者」と呼ばれていたのだ。

織田信長は尾張（愛知県）の小大名でした。

> I got the head of *Yoshimoto*!
> 義元の首を取ったぞ！

しかし桶狭間の戦いで大大名今川義元を討ち取りました。

> I've unified *Owari*. *Mino* is next.
> 尾張を統一した。次は美濃だ。

信長は、勢力を拡大していきました。

> I'll back up the shogun and rule the whole country.
> 将軍の後ろ盾として天下に号令するぞ！

信長は足利義昭を助け、京に入りました。

> The *Muromachi* shogunate was ruined.
> 室町幕府が滅びてしまった。

やがて信長は足利義昭を追放しました。

第3章　近世●天下統一と庶民の台頭

I've got a lot of stuff.
大量に手に入れたぞ。

信長は鉄砲にいち早く注目しました。

Shoot! Shoot!
撃て！撃て！

鉄砲を巧みに使って甲斐(山梨県)の武田氏を長篠の戦いで破りました。

I made commerce and industry flourish by *Rakuich-Rakuza*.
楽市・楽座を行なって、商工業も盛んにしたぞ。

信長は安土城を築き、楽市・楽座を行ないました。

The temple was set on fire.
寺に火をつけられたぞ～！

信長はキリスト教を保護する一方、比叡山や一向一揆は弾圧しました。

42. Oda Nobunaga's Ambition to Unify Japan

① *Oda Nobunaga* was a small *Daimyo* but he set out to unify Japan after winning the *Okehazama* War in 1560.
② He took control of the *Tokai* area and captured *Kyoto*, and appointed *Ashikaga Yoshiaki* as shogun.
③ Nevertheless, he kicked *Yoshiaki* out of *Kyoto* in 1573 and the *Muromachi* shogunate was ended.
④ *Nobunaga* suppressed any movements that blocked his unification. ⑤ He burned *Enryaku-ji* temple and kept down *Ikko-ikki* without mercy. ⑥ He brought *Ishiyama-hongan-ji* temple to terms. ⑦ *Nobunaga* protected Christianity partly because he wanted to set up against hostile Buddhists.
⑧ *Nobunaga* pushed new policies and took in economic power of merchants and industrialists. ⑨ *Kyoto* and *Sakai* self-governed by great merchants became under control of *Nobunaga*. ⑩ The law, *Rakuichi-Rakuza-rei*

was enacted and merchants and industrialists could do
　　制定された
business freely in the castle town of *Azuchi-jo* castle.
　　　　　　　　　　　城下町　　　　　　　　安土城
⑪*Nobunaga* carried out new policies and tried to unify
　　　　　　　実行した
Japan but he killed himself in *Honno-ji* temple in 1582
　　　　　　　自殺した　　　　　　　本能寺
due to the betrayal of his servant, *Akechi Mitsuhide*.
〜のために　　裏切り　　　　　　家臣　　明智光秀

42．織田信長の天下統一事業

①織田信長が一小大名から天下をうかがう転機となったのは、1560年の桶狭間の戦いでの勝利でした。②東海地方に勢力を広げた信長は京都へのぼり、足利義昭を将軍職につけました。
③その後義昭を1573年には京都から追放、室町幕府を滅ぼしました。
④信長は、統一を妨げる勢力には厳しく対応しました。⑤延暦寺は焼き討ちにし、一向一揆も容赦なく弾圧しました。⑥石山本願寺も降伏させました。⑦信長はキリスト教を保護しましたが、これは敵対的な仏教徒への対抗という側面もあったのです。
⑧信長は伝統にとらわれない政策を進め、商工業者の経済力の取り込みをはかりました。⑨大商人によって自治されていた京都や堺は、信長の直接支配のもとに置かれました。⑩安土城などの城下には**楽市・楽座**令が出され、誰でも自由に商工業ができるようになりました。
⑪新しい政策を実行に移し、全国統一をめざした信長でしたが、1582年、家臣の**明智光秀**に背かれて本能寺で自殺しました。

43. The Honno-ji Temple Incident (本能寺の変)

1582年

We'll make war against *Mori* in the *Chugoku* area.
中国の毛利氏を攻めるぞ！

Leave it to me.
秀吉にお任せを。

織田信長は天下統一に向け、豊臣秀吉に毛利氏攻めを命じました。

I'll go to help *Hideyoshi*.
秀吉を助けてやろう。

しかし毛利氏はなかなか降伏せず、秀吉は苦戦しました。

Mitsuhide, you go ahead.
光秀よ、先に出発せよ。

Yes, sir.
ははっ。

光秀は秀吉への援軍を率いて出発しました。

There are only a few retainers around *Nobunaga*.
信長様のまわりにはわずかな数の家来しかいないぞ。

光秀は翻意しました。

Our enemy is at *Honno-ji* temple!
敵は本能寺にあり！

光秀は途中で進路を変え、京に向かいました。

第3章 近世 ●天下統一と庶民の台頭

> Damn you, *Mitsuhide*. You betrayed me.
> おのれ光秀、裏切ったな！

光秀は本能寺の信長を襲いました。

> It's all over.
> もはやこれまで…

> I will rush back to *Kyoto*.
> 大急ぎで京都に戻るぞ！

信長は自害しました。

秀吉は信長の死の知らせを聞くと、毛利氏と和睦して京都に戻ることにしました。

> I'm beaten.
> 参った。

> I am the successor of *Nobunaga*.
> 私が信長様の後継者だ。

山崎の戦いで光秀を破りました。

光秀を倒した秀吉は天下人へ上りつめていきました。

101

44. Toyotomi Hideyoshi's Unification of Japan

① *Toyotomi Hideyoshi* took over the unification of Japan from *Nobunaga*. ② When the *Honno-ji* temple Incident happened, *Hideyoshi* was in the *Chugoku* area. ③ He went back to *Kyoto* and defeated *Akechi Mitsuhide*. ④ Next, he defeated *Shibata Katsuie*, *Nobunaga*'s powerful servant. ⑤ Therefore, he became the successor of *Nobunaga*.

⑥ *Hideyoshi* established *Osaka-jo* castle as his base. ⑦ He defeated *Chosokabe Motochika* in 1585, *Shimazu Yoshihisa* in 1587 and *Hojo Ujimasa* in 1590. ⑧ Further, he brought *Date Masamune* to his knees. ⑨ At last, he unified Japan.

⑩ *Hideyoshi* carried out *Taiko-kenchi* (the Cadastral Surveys by *Taiko*) in 1582 to rule the land and people. ⑪ As a result, peasants had a duty to pay tributes to samurai and they could not leave their land without

permission. ⑫He also carried out *Katana-gari* (the
刀狩
Order of Sword Hunt) in 1588 to take up swords and
                                     取り上げる 刀
spears from peasants. ⑬They could not rise in *Ikki* any
槍   一揆を起こす
more. ⑭*Kenchi* and *Katana-gari* divided peasants from
                                   分けた
samurai clearly and established a feudalistic class system.
                    確立した   封建的な身分制度

44. 豊臣秀吉の全国統一

①織田信長の天下統一事業を受け継いだのが、**豊臣秀吉**です。
②秀吉は、本能寺の変が起こったとき、中国地方に出陣中でした。③しかし京都へ引き返し、明智光秀を討ちました。④その後信長の有力な家臣であった柴田勝家を破りました。⑤その後秀吉は、信長の後継者の地位につきました。

⑥秀吉は、**大坂城**を築いて本拠地としました。⑦1585年に長宗我部元親、1587年に島津義久を従え、1590年に北条氏政を滅ぼしました。⑧さらに伊達政宗を屈服させました。⑨ついに秀吉は全国を統一しました。

⑩秀吉は、土地と人民を支配するため、1582年に**太閤検地**を行ないました。⑪その結果、農民は武士に対する年貢納入の義務を負わされ、土地を勝手に離れられなくなりました。⑫1588年には、農民から刀や槍などの武器を取り上げる**刀狩**をしました。⑬農民たちに一揆を起こさせないようにするためです。⑭検地と刀狩によって**兵農分離**が進み、封建的な身分制度が確立しました。

103

45. Hideyoshi's Diplomatic Policy and Sending Army to Korea

① From the middle of the 16th century, Portuguese and Spanish traded with Japan. ② This is called *Nanban trade*. ③ *Hideyoshi*, who protected *Nanban trade*, allowed Christianity at first but he thought it would block the unification of Japan and ordered the deportation of missionaries in 1587.

④ After the unification of Japan, *Hideyoshi* planned to defeat Ming. ⑤ He required Korea to obey Japan and to let his army pass through it to Ming, but Korea refused. ⑥ *Hideyoshi* gathered *Daimyo* and sent army to Korea. ⑦ This is called *Bunroku* invasion of Korea. ⑧ Japanese army occupied the capital, Hancheng, and invaded northern Korea. ⑨ Japan, however, had a hard fight because of Yi Sun-Shin's navy, the resistance of the Korean people and the reinforcements of Ming. ⑩ Japan made a cease-fire with

Korea.

⑪ *Hideyoshi* sent army to Korea again in 1597. ⑫ This is called *Keicho* invasion of Korea. ⑬ Japan continued
　　　慶長の役
invading Korea but *Hideyoshi* died the following year
　　　　　　　　　　　　　　　　　　　翌年
and Japan pulled its troops.
　　　　撤兵した

---

45. 秀吉の対外政策と朝鮮出兵

①16世紀中ごろ、ポルトガル人やスペイン人と貿易を行ないました。②これを**南蛮貿易**といいます。③南蛮貿易を保護していた豊臣秀吉は、はじめキリスト教を認めていましたが、天下統一の妨げになると考え、1587年に宣教師の国外追放を指令しました。

④秀吉は、国内統一を実現したころから、明の征服を計画していました。⑤そこで秀吉は、朝鮮に対して、日本への服属と明への通行許可を求めましたが、朝鮮はそれを断りました。⑥そこで、秀吉は大名を動員し、朝鮮に大軍を送り込みました。⑦これを**文禄の役**といいます。⑧日本軍は首都の漢城(ソウル)を占領し、朝鮮北部まで侵略しました。⑨しかし、李舜臣の水軍の活躍や、朝鮮民衆の抵抗、明の援軍などに苦しみました。⑩そこで、いったん休戦しました。

⑪秀吉は、1597年、ふたたび朝鮮に出兵を命じました。⑫これを**慶長の役**といいます。⑬日本軍は侵略を続けましたが、翌1598年、秀吉の死とともに撤退しました。

46. Momoyama Culture

① The culture of the period of *Nobunaga* and *Hideyoshi* is called *Momoyama* culture. ② Commerce and trade flourished and the production of gold and silver increased in this period. ③ New *Daimyo* and great merchants who got power and wealth lived in style. ④ *Momoyama* culture represents their power and wealth.

⑤ Stately castles that show the power of the rulers are typical of *Momoyama* culture. ⑥ These castles had high towers and grand palaces. ⑦ Pictures using gold and silver were displayed inside. ⑧ *Kano Eitoku* and *Kano Sanraku* were famous painters.

⑨ Tea ceremony was popular among *Daimyo* and great merchants. ⑩ *Sen-no-Rikyu* perfected the world of *Wabi-cha*.

⑪ People positively enjoyed their life as *Uki-yo*. ⑫ The

puppet play, *Joruri*, accompanied by *Shamisen* and
　　　　　　　浄瑠璃　　　　　　　　　　　三味線
Kabuki dance were popular.
歌舞伎踊り

⑬*Momoyama* culture came under the influence of
　　　　　　　　　　　　　　　　　　　　～の影響を受けた
European culture. ⑭Cigarettes, sponge cakes and
　　　　　　　　　　タバコ　　　　カステラ
playing cards were introduced in this period.
カルタ　　　　　　　伝えられた

46．桃山文化

①信長や秀吉の時代の文化を**桃山文化**といいます。②この時代、商業や貿易が盛んとなり、金・銀の産出が増加しました。③権力や富を手に入れた新興の大名や大商人たちは豪華な暮らしをしていました。④桃山文化は彼らの富と力を象徴する文化でした。

⑤桃山文化を代表するのは、支配者の権威を示す壮大な城です。⑥城には高くそびえる**天守閣**や豪華な御殿がつくられました。⑦内部は金銀をふんだんに使った**障壁画**で飾られました。⑧絵師としては**狩野永徳**や**狩野山楽**が知られています。

⑨大名や大商人たちの間では**茶の湯**が流行しました。⑩**千利休**は詫び茶の世界を完成しました。

⑪また、この時代は現世を浮き世として肯定的に楽しむ風潮がありました。⑫**三味線**の演奏に合わせた**浄瑠璃**が流行し、**歌舞伎踊り**が人気を集めました。

⑬ヨーロッパ文化の影響を受けているのも桃山文化の特色です。⑭タバコ、カステラ、カルタなどはこの時代に伝えられたものです。

47. The Battle of Sekigahara (関ヶ原の戦い)

> I leave *Hideyori* in your hands.
> 秀頼をよろしく頼むぞ。

> My lord.
> 殿っ！

豊臣秀吉が亡くなったとき、後継ぎの秀頼は6歳でした。

> You have an eye to becoming the next shogun.
> 家康め、天下を奪うつもりだな。

秀頼をもり立てる石田三成と徳川家康の対立が深まりました。

> I'm not fond of *Mitsunari*.
> 三成は好かん。

> Let's take the side of *Ieyasu*.
> 家康の味方をしよう。

古くからの秀吉の家臣たちは三成をきらい、家康側につきました。

> Let's join forces to defeat *Ieyasu*.
> みんなで家康を倒しましょう。

毛利氏　島津氏　宇喜多氏

三成は西国の大名を誘って家康に対抗しました。

> I'll give you a reward if you take my side.
> 私の味方になればほうびをあげますよ。

家康は各地の大名に手紙を書き、味方を増やしました。

第3章 近世 ●天下統一と庶民の台頭

1600年 関ヶ原

It seemed that the West Army had the advantage.
西軍（三成側）が有利にみえたが…

そして天下分け目の関ヶ原の戦いが始まりました。

My lord, aren't you going to war?
殿、ご出陣は？

Nope.
やめじゃ。

Defeat *Mistunari*.
三成を倒せ〜！

Oh, my god.
ひ、ひどい。

毛利氏をはじめ、西軍（三成側）に裏切りが続出しました。

どちらにつくか悩んでいた大名も多くが東軍（家康側）につきました。

The East Army has triumphed.
東軍の大勝利だぁ〜！

The *Toyotomi* family came down to only a *Daimyo*.
豊臣氏は単なる一大名になってしまいました。

戦いは東軍の勝利に終わりました。

やがて家康の天下となりました。

48. The Establishment of the Edo Shogunate

①*Tokugawa Ieyasu* strengthened his influence in the *Tokai* area and later he obeyed *Toyotomi Hideyoshi*. ②When *Hideyoshi* unified Japan in 1590, *Ieyasu* received the *Kanto* area from *Hideyoshi* and moved to *Edo* as a big *Daimyo* with 2,500,000 *goku* (the measure of capacity).

③After the death of *Hideyoshi* in 1598, *Ieyasu* became at the helm of the government. ④*Ishida Mitsunari* wanted to maintain the administration by the *Toyotomi* family and came to conflict with *Ieyasu*. ⑤Finally, in 1600, the battle of *Sekigahara* broke out between *Ieyasu* (East Army) and *Mitsunari* (West Army). ⑥*Ieyasu* won the war and *Daimyo* all over the country came to obey *Ieyasu*. ⑦After the war, *Ieyasu* got power to rule the whole country. ⑧In 1603, he established the *Edo* shogunate.

⁹Two years later, *Ieyasu* passed the title on to his son,
　　　　　　　　　　　　　　　将軍の職を〜に譲った
Hidetada. ⁱ⁰The *Toyotomi* family was still in *Osaka-jo*
秀忠
castle. ⁱⁱSo *Ieyasu* attacked *Osaka-jo* castle in 1614
　　　　　　　　　　攻めた
(the Winter War in *Osaka*), but in vain. ⁱ²At last, he
大坂冬の陣
ruined the *Toyotomi* family in the Summer War in
滅ぼした　　　　　　　　　　　　　　　　　　大坂夏の陣
Osaka in 1615.

48．江戸幕府の成立

①徳川家康は、東海地方で勢力をのばし、豊臣秀吉に従いました。②1590年、秀吉が全国統一を達成すると、関東地方を与えられ、250万石の大大名として江戸に移りました。

③1598年に秀吉が亡くなったのち、家康は政治の実権を握るようになりました。④豊臣氏による政権を維持しようとしていた石田三成は、家康と対立するようになりました。⑤1600年、家康の率いる東軍と、三成を中心とする西軍による関ヶ原の戦いが起こりました。⑥家康は勝利を得て、この結果全国の大名は家康に従うことになりました。

⑦関ヶ原の戦いののち、家康は全国支配の実権を握りました。⑧1603年には征夷大将軍に任命されて**江戸幕府**を開きました。⑨2年後、家康は将軍の職を子の秀忠に譲りました。⑩しかし、大坂城には依然として豊臣氏が残っていました。⑪そのため、1614年、大坂城を攻めました(**大坂冬の陣**)が攻めきることができませんでした。⑫翌1615年、再び大坂城を攻めて(**大坂夏の陣**)、ついに豊臣氏を滅ぼしました。

49. The System of the Rule by the Edo Shogunate

①The system of the *Edo* shogunate was almost completed by the 3rd shogun, *Tokugawa Iemitsu*. ②*Daimyo* (feudal lords) could govern their own territories. ③The *Daimyo*'s territory and the system of their rule is *Han*, and the system of rule over land and people by the shogunate and *Han* is the shogunate system. ④The biggest problem was how to control *Daimyo*. ⑤The shogunate divided *Daimyo* into three groups: *Shimpan* (feudal lords with long relationship), *Fudai* (feudal lords with middle relationship) and *Tozama* (feudal lords with short relationship). ⑥The shogun used his brain to arrange *Daimyo* to make them keep watch over one another. ⑦The shogunate enacted the Laws for the Military Houses in 1615 to restrict *Daimyo* from building castles and marriage between *Daimyo* families, and also enacted *Sankin-kotai-no-sei* (the

第3章 近世 ●天下統一と庶民の台頭

System of Mandatory Alternate Residence in *Edo* by *Daimyo*) to weaken *Daimyo*'s economic power.
⑧ Moreover, the shogunate controlled the Emperor, *Kuge*, temples and shrines. ⑨ The shogunate forbade the Emperor from getting involved in the government by the Laws Governing the imperial Court Nobility.

---

49. 江戸幕府の支配のしくみ

①江戸幕府のしくみは、3代将軍徳川家光の時代までにほぼ固まりました。②幕府は大名が領地で政治を行なうことを許しました。③大名の領地とその支配のしくみを藩といい、このような幕府と藩による土地と人民を支配するしくみを幕藩体制といいます。

④幕府が政権を維持するうえで最大の問題は、大名をいかに統制していくかということでした。⑤幕府は大名を親藩、譜代、外様に分けました。⑥大名の配置も、互いに監視させるよう巧みに工夫されました。⑦さらに、1615年には武家諸法度を発布して、築城や大名同士の結婚などについて厳しく制限し、1635年には参勤交代の制を整えて、大名の経済力を弱めようとしました。

⑧幕府の統制は天皇や公家、寺社にも及びました。⑨天皇や公家に対しては禁中並公家諸法度で政治に関わることを禁止しました。

50. The Shuin-sen Trade (The Vermilion-Seal Certificate Trade) and the Japanese Towns

①From the end of the 16th century, Japanese people frequently went abroad. ②Many merchants went to Southeast Asia. ③*Hideyoshi* protected these merchants and encouraged them to trade.

④*Ieyasu* tried to energize the trade with neighboring countries. ⑤Therefore, he gave the *Daimyo* in *Kyushu* and great merchants *Shuin-jo* to travel abroad. ⑥*Shuin-jo* was a document sealed in vermilion by the ruler and the trade done by *Shuin-sen* (vermilion-seal ships) was called *Shuin-sen* trade.

⑦A lot of Japanese people came to live in the cities in Southeast Asia such as Luzon, Annam and Siam, and they built self-governing Japanese towns all around there.

⑧Among the Japanese people who went abroad, *Yamada Nagamasa* is the most famous. ⑨He was a

boss of a Japanese town and was given an important
　長
post, *Taishu*, by the royal family of Siam.
　位　　太守　　　　　シャムの王室

⑩*Shuin-sen* trade ended at the beginning of the 17th century because the shogunate enforced strict control
　　　　　　　　　　　　　　　　　　　　～の取り締まりを厳しくした
over Christianity.
　　　キリスト教

50. 朱印船貿易と日本町

①16世紀末ごろから、日本人の海外進出は盛んになりました。②東南アジアに渡る商人も多くなりました。③豊臣秀吉はこれらの商人を保護し、貿易を奨励しました。

④徳川家康も、近隣の諸国との貿易を盛んにしようとしました。⑤そのため、九州の大名や大商人に海外渡航を許可する**朱印状**を与えました。⑥朱印状とは、支配者の朱印が押された公文書のことで、朱印状を与えられた朱印船によって行なわれた貿易を**朱印船貿易**といいます。

⑦ルソン(現在のフィリピン)、アンナン(ベトナム)、シャム(タイ)などの東南アジアには、日本人がたくさん住みつくようになり、自治制を敷いた**日本町**が各地につくられるようになりました。

⑧渡航した日本人のなかで、特に有名な人物は**山田長政**です。⑨彼は日本町の長でしたが、シャムの王室で重く用いられ、太守(長官)となりました。

⑩朱印船貿易は、17世紀の前半、キリスト教の取り締まりが厳しくなり、廃止されました。

51. The Ban on Christianity and the National Seclusion

① Initially, the *Edo* shogunate tried to develop trade. ② As a result, trade flourished and Christianity spread through missionaries at the same time, but Christianity threatened to collapse the system of the shogunate which was based on *Shi-no-ko-sho* (the class system that ranks Samurai at the top, followed by peasants, craftsmen and merchants). ③ Therefore, the shogunate banned Christianity.

④ The shogunate enacted the anti-Christian edict in its direct territories in 1612 and applied it to all over the country the following year.

⑤ In 1637, *Shimabara-Amakusa-ikki* broke out. ⑥ *Kirishitan* (Christians) peasants rose in this *ikki* (riot) but it was broken down. ⑦ After that, the shogunate put the people through the stamping on a picture of Christ, listed all the people on the list,

Shumon-aratame-cho, as Buddhists, and forced them
宗門改帳　　　　　　　　　　　　　　仏教徒
to belong to temples. ⑧This system is called *Terauke-*
　～に属する　　　　　　　　　　　　　　　　　　寺請制度
seido.

⑨The shogunate banned the Portuguese entry into Japan
　　　　　　　　　　　　　　　ポルトガル人の　来航
in 1639. ⑩This policy of the shogunate is called *Sakoku*
　　　　　　　　政策　　　　　　　　　　　　　　　　鎖国
(the National Seclusion) and lasted for 200 years.
　　　　　　　　　　　　　　　　　　続いた　　　200年間

---

51. 禁教と鎖国

①江戸幕府は成立当初、貿易の発展に努めました。②その結果、貿易は盛んになり、キリスト教が来日した宣教師を通して広まっていきましたが、キリスト教の信仰は、士農工商の身分制度の上に成り立っている幕府のしくみを崩壊させる危険がありました。③そのため、幕府はキリスト教を禁止していきました。
④1612年、幕府は直轄領に禁教令を出し、翌年にはこれを全国に広めました。
⑤1637年、九州で島原・天草一揆が起こりました。⑥これは、キリシタンを中心とする農民が起こした一揆でしたが、鎮圧されました。⑦幕府はこののち、踏絵（絵踏）を行ない、すべての人民を仏教徒として宗門改帳に記し、いずれかの寺の信徒としました。⑧この制度を寺請制度といいます。
⑨1639年、幕府はポルトガル人の来航を禁止しました。⑩このような幕府の政策を鎖国といい、以後200年にわたって続くことになりました。

52. The Three Capitals: Edo, Osaka and Kyoto

①The *Edo* shogunate and *Han* developed new fields by building irrigation canals and reclaiming land by drainage. ②Improvement and invention of farm tools increased agricultural production. ③In this period, traffic networks were improved and the flow of goods was increased, so cities all over the country flourished.

④Among them, *Edo*, *Osaka* and *Kyoto* prospered and they were called the three capitals, *San-to*.
⑤*Edo* was called the shogun's home territory and flourished as the center of the government.
⑥*Osaka* was called the kitchen of Japan and was a big commercial city. ⑦*Han* all over the country built storerooms there and sold rice and local products.
⑧Regular shipping routes were introduced between *Osaka* and *Edo*, and commodities people in *Edo* needed were transported from *Osaka*.

⑨The Emperor and *Kuge* (court nobles) lived in *Kyoto*.
　　　天皇　　　　　　　公家
⑩There were many temples and shrines. ⑪Traditional
　　　　　　　　　　　寺院　　　　神社　　　　　　　伝統的な
handicraft industry typical of *Nishijin* brocade and
手工業　　　　　　　～に代表される　西陣織
Kyoto dye goods flourished.
京染

---

52. 三都～江戸・大坂・京都

①江戸幕府や各藩は、土地の開墾に力を入れ、用水路をつくったり、干拓したりして、新田開発を進めました。②また、農具の改良や発明があり、農業生産は増えました。③この時期は、交通路が整備され、商品の流通が盛んになり、各地の都市は栄えました。④特に、**江戸・大坂・京都**は繁栄し、**三都**と呼ばれました。

⑤**江戸**は「**将軍のお膝元**」と呼ばれ、政治の中心地として繁栄しました。

⑥**大坂**は「**天下の台所**」と呼ばれる大商業都市でした。⑦全国の藩が**蔵屋敷**を建て、年貢米や特産物を販売しました。⑧大坂と江戸との間には定期航路が開かれ、江戸の住民の生活に必要な物資が大坂から送られるようになりました。

⑨**京都**には天皇や公家が居住していました。⑩多くの寺院や神社がありました。⑪**西陣織**や**京染**に代表される、伝統的な手工業が盛んでした。

53. The Government by Tokugawa Tsunayoshi and the Shotoku-no-chi

①The 5th shogun, *Tokugawa Tsunayoshi* (徳川綱吉), was a bookman (学問好き) and tried to govern the country by Confucian teachings (儒学の教え). ②This is called *Bunchi-shugi* (文治主義) (the principles of civilian governmment). ③Nevertheless, at the end of his era, he indulged in luxury (ぜいたくにふけった) and the shogunate gradually faced (直面した) financial difficulties (財政難).

④*Tsunayoshi* debased the currency (貨幣の質を落とした) and issued (発行した) more coins to improve (改善する) his finances. ⑤This policy caused (ひき起こした) a boost in prices (物価の上昇) and disrupted (混乱させた) the economy. ⑥On the other hand, he enacted (制定した) the law, *Shorui-awaremi-no-rei* (生類憐みの令), to prohibit (禁じる) the killing (殺生) of animals. ⑦*Tsunayoshi* was called *Inu-kubo* (犬公方) (dog-lover shogun) because he made the most of (〜を大切にする) dogs among others. ⑧This period is called the *Genroku* period (元禄時代).

⑨*Ienobu* (家宣) became the shogun after *Tsunayoshi* and repealed (廃止した) the *Shorui-awaremi-no-rei* and selected (登用した) *Arai* (新井白石)

Hakuseki to carry out political reform.

⑩ *Arai Hakuseki* minted good coins and tried to control price increases. ⑪ He restricted *Nagasaki* trade to prevent the outflow of gold and silver and to re-establish the economy of the shogunate.

53. 徳川綱吉の政治と正徳の治

①第5代将軍徳川綱吉は学問好きであり、儒学の教えを広めることで、世の中を治めようとしました。②この考えを文治主義といいます。③しかし、治世の後半になると、生活がぜいたくになり、幕府はしだいに財政難に陥りました。

④このため、綱吉は貨幣の質を落として、その分貨幣の数量を多く発行し、財政の不足を補おうとしました。⑤この政策は物価の上昇をひき起こし、経済を混乱させることになりました。

⑥さらに、綱吉は、生類憐みの令を出し、生き物の殺生を禁じました。⑦なお、綱吉は、生き物のなかでも特に犬を大切にしたため、「犬公方」といわれました。⑧綱吉が将軍であった時代を元禄時代といいます。

⑨綱吉にかわって将軍となった家宣は、生類憐みの令を廃止するとともに、新井白石を登用し、政治改革にあたらせました。

⑩新井白石は質の良い貨幣を発行して、物価の上昇を抑えようとしました。⑪さらに長崎貿易を制限して、金や銀の流出を抑え、財政の立て直しをはかりました。

54. Genroku Culture

① In the *Genroku* period, society was stabilized, and commerce and industry developed. ② Townspeople produced a vigorous and colorful culture. ③ This culture is called *Genroku* culture.

④ *Ihara Saikaku*, *Chikamatsu Monzaemon* and *Matsuo Basho* were famous writers in the *Genroku* period.

⑤ *Ihara Saikaku* wrote *The Man Who Spent His Life at Love-Making* and so on, describing everything about the social situation and mode of life in this period. ⑥ These works are called *Ukiyo-zoshi*.

⑦ *Chikamatsu Monzaemon* wrote scripts of the puppet show, *Ningyo-joruri*, and Kabuki, describing tragedy in the world of love and duty. ⑧ *Ningyo-joruri* gained popularity by the narration of *Takemoto Gidayu*.

⑨ *Matsuo Basho* was a haiku (17-syllable Japanese poem) poet and gave haiku great artistic value. ⑩ He traveled all over the country and wrote excellent (優れた) works, such as *The Narrow Road to the Interior* (『奥の細道』).

⑪ *Ogata Korin* (尾形光琳) completed (完成させた) colorful decorative paintings (装飾画).

⑫ *Hishikawa Moronobu* (菱川師宣) painted ukiyoe (浮世絵) such as *Mikaeri-bijin-zu* (見返り美人図) (Beauty Looking Back).

---

54. 元禄文化

①元禄時代は、世の中が安定し、商工業が発達しました。②こうした中で、町人は、活気ある華やかな文化を生み出しました。③この文化を**元禄文化**といいます。

④井原西鶴・近松門左衛門・松尾芭蕉は、元禄時代の文学を代表する人物です。

⑤井原西鶴は、現実の世相や風俗を描き、『**好色一代男**』などの作品を残しました。⑥これらの作品は、**浮世草子**と呼ばれています。

⑦近松門左衛門は、**人形浄瑠璃**や歌舞伎の脚本を書き、義理や人情の世界の悲劇を描きました。⑧人形浄瑠璃は竹本義太夫の語りによって人気を得ました。

⑨松尾芭蕉は俳人で、**俳諧**の芸術的価値を高めました。⑩また日本各地を旅し、『**奥の細道**』など優れた作品を残しました。

⑪**尾形光琳**は、華やかな**装飾画**を完成させました。⑫**菱川師宣**は、『見返り美人図』などの**浮世絵**を描きました。

55. The Reform of Kyoho

① In the *Genroku* period, the flow of goods increased and a money economy developed. ② Therefore, the shogunate and *Han* that were based on self-supporting economy got into financial trouble. ③ In the meantime, *Tokugawa Yoshimune* became the 8th shogun in 1716. ④ *Yoshimune* stopped the government by associates of shogun. ⑤ He took the lead in political reform. ⑥ This political reform lasted about 30 years and is called the reform of *Kyoho*.

⑦ The largest chore in this reform was setting the shogunate's finances in order. ⑧ *Yoshimune* himself led a simple life and became a model for samurai. ⑨ He made *Daimyo* give up a certain amount of rice instead of a reduction of the burden of *Sankin-kotai*. ⑩ This system is called *Agemai-no-sei*.

⑪ *Yoshimune* carried out the town government as well.

⑫ He installed the complaint box, *Meyasu-bako*, to reflect the opinion of people in the government. ⑬ He enacted the criminal law, *Kujikata-osadamegaki*, for trials and punishments.

55. 享保の改革

①元禄時代には、商品の流通が活発になり、貨幣経済が発達してきました。②このため、従来の自給自足的な経済の上に立つ幕府や藩は財政難に陥りました。③こうしたなか、1716年、第8代将軍となったのが徳川吉宗です。

④吉宗は、側近に政治を任せませんでした。⑤自らが先頭に立って政治改革を推し進めていきました。⑥およそ30年にわたるこの政治改革を享保の改革といいます。

⑦改革の中心は幕府財政の立て直しでした。⑧将軍自ら質素倹約を実行して、武士に模範を示しました。⑨大名に対しては参勤交代を緩めるかわりに、一定量の米を献上させました。⑩これを上げ米の制といいます。

⑪吉宗は町政にも努力しました。⑫まず、目安箱を設けて庶民の意見を政治に反映させようとしました。⑬さらに、裁判や刑の基準となる公事方御定書を定めました。

56. The Government by Tanuma Okitsugu

①In the 10th shogun, *Tokugawa Ieharu* era, *Roju* (senior councilor) *Tanuma Okitsugu* was at the helm of the shogunate.

②The chore in *Okitsugu*'s reform was rebuilding the shogunate finances. ③He tried to rebuild them by increasing the private sectors' economic power. ④First, he authorized the Licensed Commercial Association and imposed a tax on them. ⑤Second, he tried to develop new fields by draining. ⑥Third, he developed *Ezo-chi* to trade with Russia and eased trade restriction in *Nagasaki* to give an impulse to trade. ⑦This reform was novel but great merchants came to have cozy relations with shogunate officials, and bribery prevailed. ⑧It caused political confusion. ⑨On the other hand, in 1783, Mt. *Asama* erupted and it was part of the reason for the *Temmei* famine. ⑩This resulted in *Hyakusho-ikki* (peasant riot) in rural areas and *Uchikowashi* (urban riot) in urban areas. ⑪The shogunate and *Han* couldn't take effective action against them. ⑫Therefore, strong criticisms were made against *Okitsugu* and he fell from power in 1786.

56. 田沼意次の政治

①第10代将軍徳川家治の時代になると、老中田沼意次が幕府の実権を握るようになりました。
②意次の改革が目指したのは、幕府の財政を再建することでした。③意次は、民間の経済力を伸ばしていくことによって、幕府の財政を再建しようとしました。
④意次は株仲間を公認し、税を納めさせました。⑤また、干拓によって新田開発を進めようとしました。⑥さらに、蝦夷地(北海道)を開拓してロシアと交易しようとしたり、長崎貿易の制約を緩和して、貿易を盛んにしようとしました。
⑦こうした意次の改革は、斬新なものでしたが、幕府の役人と大商人との癒着を生み、わいろが広まりました。⑧やがて、政治が混乱するようになりました。⑨また、1783年に浅間山で大噴火が起こり、天明のききんの一因となりました。⑩この結果、農村では百姓一揆が、都市では打ちこわしが起こるようになりました。⑪幕府や藩では、こうした情勢に対して有効な対策を打ち出すことができませんでした。⑫このため、意次に対する批判は激しくなり、1786年、意次は失脚しました。

57. The Reform of Kansei

① *Tokugawa Ienari* became the 11th shogun in 1787, and *Matsudaira Sadanobu* became the *Roju* and carried out the shogunate government. ② He carried out political reform. ③ This reform is called the reform of *Kansei*. ④ *Sadanobu* wanted to end the political turmoil and set shogunate finances in order. ⑤ He also tried to tone down the giddy mood of samurai and the common people. ⑥ *Sadanobu* forbade peasants from working away from home to restore farm villages. ⑦ He forced *Hatamoto* (direct retainers of the shogun) and *Gokenin* (shogun's followers) to lead a frugal life. ⑧ He also made *Daimyo* save a certain amount of rice, and made peasants build storehouses to save rice in preparation for famine. ⑨ This is called *Kakoi-mai*. ⑩ Learning except *Shushi-gaku* (the teaching of Chu Hsi) was banned. ⑪ This is called *Kansei-igaku-no-kin*.

⑫The shogunate screened books to check criticisms and caricatures against the shogunate, and came down hard on public morals.
⑬*Sadanobu*'s reform was strict and faced opposition from the people, so he fell from power in six years.

57. 寛政の改革

①1787年、第11代将軍に徳川家斉がついたときに老中となり、幕府の政治を動かしたのが松平定信です。②定信は政治改革を推進しました。③定信による幕府政治の改革を寛政の改革といいます。

④定信は混乱した政治を改め、財政を立て直すことを目指しました。⑤さらにゆるんだ武士や民衆の気風を引き締めようとしました。

⑥定信は、荒廃した農村を復興させるため、農民が出稼ぎに出ることを禁止しました。⑦一方、旗本や御家人に対しては、倹約を求めました。⑧また、ききんに備えるため、大名に対して一定量の米を蓄えさせ、農村には倉を建てさせて米を保存させようとしました。⑨これを囲米といいます。

⑩学問の面では、朱子学以外の学問を禁止しました。⑪これを寛政異学の禁といいます。⑫出版を統制し、幕府に対する批判や風刺を抑え、風俗の取り締まりを厳しくしました。

⑬こうした定信の改革は厳しいものであったため、民衆の反発を招いて6年で失脚しました。

58. The Change in Farm Villages, Ikki and Uchikowashi

①The commodity economy spread to farm villages, so a lot of peasants grew and sold commercial crops. ②Hence, in farm villages, a self-supporting economy changed to a money economy. ③Some peasants became rich and became *Jinushi* (land owner). ④People who gave up their land and became tenant farmers increased. ⑤After the reform of *Kyoho*, the shogunate and *Han* collected tributes more strictly to get over their financial troubles. ⑥Therefore, many peasants worked away from home in cities and devastated farmland increased. ⑦Famines frequently occurred. ⑧There were three big famines in the *Edo* period: the *Kyoho* famine in 1732, the *Temmei* famine from 1782 to 1787 and the *Tempo* famine from 1833 to 1839.

⑨Peasants required *Ryoshu* (lord of the manor) to reduce their tributes. ⑩They bore arms and rose in an

Ikki when *Ryoshu* refused their demands. ⑪This is
　　　　　　　　　　拒否した　　　要求
called *Hyakusho-ikki* (peasant riot). ⑫In cities, goods
　　　　百姓一揆　　　　　　　　　　　　　　　商品
became in short supply and the price for rice rose
　　　　　不足した　　　　　　　　　米価
sharply. ⑬Therefore, poor people attacked merchants.
高騰した　　　　　　　　　　　　　襲った
⑭This is called *Uchikowashi* (urban riot).
　　　　　　　打ちこわし

58．農村の変化と一揆・打ちこわし

①農村では、商品経済が広まったため、商品作物を栽培して販売しようとする農家が多くなりました。②こうして、農村の経済は、自給自足経済から**貨幣経済**へと変化しました。③このようななか、裕福になった農民が現れ、地主になる者もいました。④その一方で、土地を手放して小作人となる者が増加しました。⑤享保の改革以降、幕府や藩は財政難を解消するため、年貢の取り立てをいっそう厳しくしました。⑥このため、農民が都市に出稼ぎに出るようになり、荒れたままの耕地が増えました。⑦また、ききんがたびたび起こりました。⑧1732年の享保のききん、1782年から87年にかけての天明のききん、1833年から39年にかけての天保のききんは江戸時代の三大ききんといわれています。

⑨農民たちは、年貢の引き下げを求めて領主に訴えました。⑩受け入れられない場合は武装して一揆を起こしました。⑪これを**百姓一揆**といいます。⑫また、都市では商品が不足したり、米価が高騰しました。⑬そのため貧しい人々が中心となって商人を襲いました。⑭これを**打ちこわし**といいます。

59. The Access of Foreign Ships

①During Japan's national seclusion, there were many changes in the world. ②In Britain and France, the absolute monarchies were defeated by the people's revolutions and modern societies were born. ③The ships of Russia, the U.S. and Britain appeared in seas close to Japan.

④In 1792, Russia's ambassador, Laksman, dropped into *Nemuro* and required Japan to open trade. ⑤The shogunate refused his request and keep a close watch on northern Japan.

⑥In 1808, the British warship, the Phaeton, arrived in *Nagasaki*. ⑦After that, ships of Britain and the U.S. appeared one after another.

⑧In 1825, the shogunate enacted the decree for expelling foreign ships to fight off foreign ships. ⑨*Watanabe Kazan*, *Takano Choei* and others criticized

the shogunate's seclusion policy as going against the
時代の潮流に逆らうものとして
tide of the times. ⑩ The shogunate punished them. ⑪ This
処罰した
incident is called *Bansha-no-goku*.
蛮社の獄

59. 外国船の接近

①日本が鎖国を続けている間に、世界の情勢は大きく変化していきました。②イギリスやフランスでは、市民革命によって絶対王政が倒れ、近代社会が開かれました。③やがてロシアやアメリカ、イギリスなどの船が日本の沿岸に現れるようになりました。

④1792年、ロシアの使節ラクスマンが北海道の根室に来航し、日本との通商を求めました。⑤幕府はロシアの通商要求を拒否するとともに、日本の北方の警備を厳重に行なうようになりました。

⑥1808年には、イギリスの軍艦フェートン号が長崎に入港しました(フェートン号事件)。⑦この後も、イギリス船やアメリカ船が日本近海に続々と現れました。

⑧1825年幕府は異国船打払令を出し、外国船の撃退を命じました。⑨渡辺崋山や高野長英らは、幕府の鎖国政策を世界の潮流に沿わないものとして批判しました。⑩それゆえ、幕府は彼らを処罰しました。⑪これを蛮社の獄といいます。

60. Kasei Culture

①In the 11th shogun *Tokugawa Ienari* era, the center of culture moved from *Kamigata* (*Kyoto* and *Osaka*) to *Edo*, which achieved remarkable economic development. ②The mass culture ripened and became diverse. ③This is called *Kasei* culture.

④People became familiar with literature in this period. ⑤*Jippensha Ikku*'s comedy, *Up the Eastern Sea Circuit on Shank's Mare*, was popular. ⑥*Takizawa Bakin*'s *The Biographies of Eight Dogs* was widely read. ⑦As for *Haikai* (haiku poem), *Yosa Buson* and *Kobayashi Issa* were popular among people. ⑧*Kyoka* (satirical *tanka* poem) and *Senryu* (humorous poem) spread among people.

⑨Ukiyoe was mainly painted. ⑩*Suzuki Harunobu*'s color prints called *Nishiki-e* were very popular and ukiyoe was at its best. ⑪There was *Kitagawa Utamaro*'s portrait, *Bijin-ga*. ⑫*Katsushika Hokusai*'s the Thirty-six views of Mt. *Fuji* and *Utagawa Hiroshige*'s the Fifty-three Stages on the *Tokai-do* road were famous landscape paintings. ⑬In *Yakusha-e* (portrait of actors), *Toshusai Sharaku* was popular.

---

60. 化政文化

①第11代将軍徳川家斉の時代になると、文化の中心は京都・大坂の上方から経済発展の著しい江戸に移りました。②町人文化はいっそう成熟するとともに多様化しました。③この文化を**化政文化**といいます。

④文学は、広く民衆のものとなりました。⑤小説では、十返舎一九の『東海道中膝栗毛』が滑稽本として人気がありました。⑥滝沢馬琴の『南総里見八犬伝』も多くの人々に読まれました。⑦俳諧では、与謝蕪村や小林一茶が民衆の間で親しまれました。⑧また、狂歌や川柳が広く民衆の間に広まりました。

⑨絵画では、浮世絵が中心でした。⑩鈴木春信の多色刷りの版画は錦絵と呼ばれてもっとも人気があり、浮世絵は全盛期を迎えました。⑪美人画では喜多川歌麿の肖像画があります。⑫風景画では『富嶽三十六景』を描いた**葛飾北斎**や、『東海道五十三次』を描いた**歌川広重**が有名です。⑬役者絵では**東洲斎写楽**が人気がありました。

61. The Reform of Tempo

① In the 1830s, the *Tempo* famine occurred and many people died from starvation. ② *Hyakusho-ikki* and *Uchikowashi* broke out all over the country. ③ On the other hand, ships of Russia, Britain and the U.S. came close to Japan and required Japan to open the country. ④ *Roju*, *Mizuno Tadakuni*, carried out political reform under these circumstances. ⑤ This is called the reform of *Tempo*.

⑥ First, *Tadakuni* enacted the thrift Ordinance to stop the luxury life led by samurai and the people. ⑦ Second, he enacted the decree, *Hitogaeshi-no-ho*, to rebuild the devastated farmland and forced peasants in *Edo* to return home. ⑧ Last, he enacted the decree, *Jochi-rei*, to take up the territory of *Daimyo* and *Hatamoto* (the direct retainers of shogun) around *Osaka* and *Edo*, and to get over the financial troubles. ⑨ This law didn't

succeed due to opposition by *Daimyo* and *Hatamoto*.
成功する　～のために　反対
⑩ *Tadakuni* fell from power and failed in the reform.
　　　　失脚した　　　　　　　～に失敗した

61. 天保の改革

①1830年代になると、天保の大ききんに見舞われ、餓死するものが続出しました。②そのため、百姓一揆や打ちこわしが各地で起こりました。③さらに、日本の近海には、ロシアやイギリス、アメリカなどの船が接近し、日本に開国を迫ってきていました。④こうした情勢の中で、政治改革を行なったのが老中水野忠邦です。⑤忠邦の改革を天保の改革といいます。
⑥忠邦は倹約令を出し、ぜいたくになってきた武士や庶民の生活を引き締めました。⑦ついで、荒廃した農村を再建するために人返しの法を出し、江戸に出稼ぎにきていた農民を帰郷させました。⑧さらに上知(上地)令を出し、江戸や大坂の周辺にある大名や旗本の領地を幕府の直轄領として、財政難を切り抜けようとしました。⑨しかしこれは大名や旗本の反対にあって成功しませんでした。⑩忠邦は失脚し、改革は失敗に終わりました。

Horse 馬

Too Sophisticated?
カッコよすぎ?

A samurai in full armor rides a horse and fights in the battlefield. This is a scene everybody, not only movie fans and historical film fans, has seen. Oh, no, there is something wrong with this scene. What's wrong? The horse is! It is too big.

In the Japanese Islands, there were wild horses about 20 thousand years ago. But their height was about 1.2 meters, just like the donkeys we know today, and they were not good for riding.

The custom of horse riding might have spread in the 5th century. Some ancient clay figures placed on *Ko-fun* at that time were horse-shaped and some funerary goods were harnesses.

The reason why the custom of horse riding spread in this period was that horses from the northern part of the Chinese continent were introduced to Japan at that time. Those horses were about 1.4 meters high and good for riding. On the other hand, Japanese horses grew very little in size for a long time.

So, we feel there is something wrong with the scene that a feudal warlord is riding a thoroughbred or an Arab horse whose height is no less than 1.6 meters.

よろい・かぶとを身につけた武士が馬にまたがり、戦場を駆けめぐる。映画ファン・時代劇ファンのみならず、誰もが見たことのあるシーン。いや、ちょっと違うぞ！ 何が違うって？ ウマです。ウマが大きすぎるのです。

日本列島にも、野生のウマはいました。2万年前のことですが、大きさ(体高)はロバぐらいで、そう1.2mぐらい。あまり乗馬に適しているとはいえません。

5世紀になって乗馬の風習が広がったようで、古墳の上に並べてあるはにわにウマの形をしたものが出現したり、副葬品に馬具が納められたりしました。

5世紀に乗馬が広まったのは、中国大陸の北方のウマが伝えられ、乗用にたえるウマになったからです。このころのウマ、大きさは1.4mぐらい。このあと、日本のウマはごくわずかずつしか大型化しませんでした。

だから、戦国時代の武将が、1.6mもあろうかというサラブレッドやアラブ馬に乗っているのはどこか違うぞ、と言いたくなるのです。

Chapter 4
The Present Age

Japan
in the International
Community

第4章 近代
国際社会の中の日本

62. The Perry's Arrival

① The U.S. planned to open Japan to use it as a stopping point for whaling ships and trading ships to China.
② Commodore Perry dropped into *Uraga* in 1853. ③ The people in Japan were surprised at and afraid of the ships and called them *Kuro-Fune*(black ships).
④ Perry handed the shogunate a message from the President of the U.S. ⑤ The shogunate reported it to the Court and asked the opinions of *Daimyo*.
⑥ Perry came to *Edo* bay again the following year. ⑦ The shogunate didn't want to make war against the U.S. because it knew the result of the Opium War. ⑧ So it made a treaty with the U.S. ⑨ This treaty is called Treaty of Peace and Amity between the U.S. and the Empire of Japan. ⑩ It made Japan open *Shimoda* port and *Hakodate* port and accept the requirement to supply food, water and coal to the ships of the U.S.

⑪ In 1858, *Tairo, Ii Naosuke,* made the Harris Treaty
　　　　　　大老　　井伊直弼　　　　　　　　　　　日米修好通商条約
with the U.S. and promised to open five ports. ⑫ This
　　　　　　　　　約束した
was an unequal treaty, which conceded exterritoriality
　　　不平等条約　　　　　　　　　　　　認める　　　　　治外法権
and had no customs autonomy of Japan.
　　　　　　　関税自主権

---

62. ペリー来航

①アメリカは、捕鯨船や中国との貿易船の中継地として日本を開国させようと計画しました。②1853年、ペリーが浦賀（神奈川県）に入港しました。③人々は、これを「黒船」と呼んで、驚き、また恐れました。

④ペリーは、大統領の国書を幕府に差し出しました。⑤幕府は、これを朝廷に報告するとともに、諸大名の意見を求めました。

⑥ペリーは、翌年、ふたたび来航し、江戸湾に侵入しました。⑦幕府は、アヘン戦争のような事態になることをおそれ、戦争を望みませんでした。⑧そしてアメリカと条約を結びました。⑨これを**日米和親条約**といいます。⑩下田（静岡県）と箱館（北海道）の2港を開き、アメリカ船に食料、水、石炭を供給することを認めました。

⑪1858年、**大老井伊直弼**は**日米修好通商条約**を結び、5港を開く約束をしました。⑫この条約は**領事裁判権（治外法権）**を認め、**関税自主権**をもたない不平等条約でした。

63. The Unification of the Court and the Shogunate, and the Imperialist's Antiforeigner

①Trade with foreign countries invited a price rise and people lived a hard life. ②Hence, the antiforeigner movement began. ③They opposed opening the country and insisted that Japan beat off foreigners by military means. ④It gradually became the imperialist's antiforeigner movement. ⑤*Ii Naosuke* clamped down on this movement and was assassinated in front of *Sakurada-mon* (one of the gates in *Edo-jo* castle).
⑥*Roju, Ando Nobumasa*, carried out the government after *Naosuke*. ⑦He wanted to unite the Court with the shogunate (*Ko-bu* gattai) to check the movement.
⑧*Choshu-han* held the imperialist's antiforeigner movement and fired a gun at a foreign ship in 1863, but it was attacked in retaliation by the combined fleet.
⑨*Choshu-han* got thrown out of *Kyoto* by *Satsuma-han* and *Aizu-han* which supported the Unification of

the Court and the shogunate. ⑩ In 1864, <u>the shogunate</u>
<u>幕府</u>
attacked *Choshu-han* and it <u>gave in</u>.
<u>降伏した</u>
⑪ In 1862, a British man was killed by *Satsuma-han*(*Namamugi-jiken*). ⑫ British warship <u>came to make</u>
<u>報復しに来た</u>
<u>a countercharge</u> the following year(*Satsu-Ei-sensou*).

63. 公武合体と尊王攘夷

①外国と貿易が始まると物価は上昇し、国民の生活が苦しくなりました。②このため、**攘夷運動**が起こりました。③攘夷を支持する人々は、開国に反対し、武力で外敵を打ち払えと主張しました。④それはやがて、**尊王攘夷運動**へと発展しました。⑤**井伊直弼**はこの運動を弾圧しましたが、江戸城桜田門外で暗殺されました(**桜田門外の変**)。

⑥直弼のあと幕政をとったのは老中安藤信正でした。⑦信正は尊王攘夷運動をおさえようと**公武合体**を進めました。

⑧**長州藩**では尊王攘夷運動が活発で、1863年、外国船に発砲しましたが、連合艦隊に報復攻撃を受けました。⑨さらに、公武合体派の薩摩藩・会津藩(福島県)により、尊王攘夷派の長州藩は京都から追放されました(**八月十八日の政変**)。⑩1864年、幕府は長州藩を攻撃し、長州藩は降伏しました。

⑪一方、**薩摩藩**では1862年、イギリス人を殺傷しました(**生麦事件**)。⑫翌年イギリスの報復を受けました(**薩英戦争**)。

64. The Satsu-Cho Alliance and the To-baku Movement

① *Takasugi Shinsaku* and others seized the initiative in the *Choshu-han*. ② They thought that they should defeat the shogunate and establish a strong unified country which could stand against foreign countries. ③ *Satsuma-han* led by *Okubo Toshimichi* and *Saigo Takamori* strengthened its power with the help of Britain. ④ *Satsuma-han* and *Choshu-han* were in conflict with each other but *Sakamoto Ryoma* persuaded them to come together to overthrow the shogunate. ⑤ Hence, *Satsu-Cho* alliance was formed. ⑥ The shogunate made *Choshu-han* give in in 1864 and ordered it to scale back its territory. ⑦ Nevertheless, *Choshu-han* disobeyed the order. ⑧ The shogunate went on an expedition to *Choshu* with some other *Han* but got defeated. ⑨ The loss of the expedition to *Choshu* exposed the diminishing authority of the shogunate.

⑩The economic disorders and the political uncertainty
　経済の混乱　　　　　　　　　　　　　　　政情不安
led to social unrest and the people looked forward to
　　　社会不安　　　　　　　　　　　　　～を期待した
social reform. ⑪In 1867, the people made a fuss,
世直し　　　　　　　　　　　　　　　　騒ぎを起こした
dancing madly and shouting "*Eejanaika.*"
　　　　　　　　　　　　　　　ええじゃないか

64. 薩長同盟と討幕運動

①長州藩では、高杉晋作らが藩の主導権を握りました。②彼らは幕府を倒して強い統一国家をつくり、外国と対抗できる強い国にする必要があると考えました。③薩摩藩も、大久保利通や西郷隆盛らが中心となって、イギリスの援助を受けて藩の力を強めていきました。④薩長両藩は対立していましたが、坂本龍馬は、両藩が協力して倒幕を目指すよう説得しました。⑤これにより薩長同盟が成立しました。

⑥幕府は1864年に長州藩を屈服させ、領地の削減を命じていました。⑦しかし、長州藩は幕府の命令に従いませんでした。⑧そのため、幕府は諸藩に命じて長州征伐を行ないましたが、敗北に終わりました。⑨長州征伐の失敗は、幕府の権威が衰えてきたことを示す結果となりました。

⑩経済が混乱してくると、政情不安もあって社会不安が増大し、世直しを期待する声が大きくなりました。⑪1867年には「ええじゃないか」と叫び、乱舞する騒ぎが起こりました。

65. The Return of Power Back to the Emperor and the Restoration

① *Tokugawa Yoshinobu* became the 15th shogun in 1866 but the ex-head of *Tosa-han*, *Yamanouchi Toyoshige*, found that *Satsuma-han* and *Choshu-han* planned to overthrow the shogunate by military means and advised *Yoshinobu* to return the administration to the Court. ② *Yoshinobu* followed his advice on October 14, 1867. ③ This is called *Taisei-hokan*.
④ *Saigo Takamori* and *Okubo Toshimichi* of *Satsuma-han* and a *Kuge*, *Iwakura Tomomi*, worked on the Court to overthrow the shogunate. ⑤ On December 9, 1867, the Court enacted the decree, *Osei-fukko-no-dai-gorei*, to express that it would put an end to the shogunate and carry out a government with the Emperor at its center. ⑥ In this way, the *Edo* shogunate was ruined.
⑦ The new government took a hard line on the

<u>*Tokugawa* family</u> and demanded the return of their
territory. ⁸The new government army moved east and
forced them to give up *Edo-jo* castle without a blow.
⁹In the following year, it brought the ex-shogunate
army to terms at the castle, *Goryokaku*, in *Hakodate*.
⑩This civil war is called the *Boshin* war.

65. 大政奉還と王政復古

①1866年、徳川慶喜が第15代将軍となりましたが、前土佐藩主の山内豊信(容堂)は、薩摩・長州の両藩が武力による倒幕の計画を進めていることを知り、慶喜に政権を朝廷に返すよう進言しました。②慶喜はこれに従い、1867年10月14日、政権を朝廷に返上しました。③これを大政奉還といいます。
④薩摩藩の西郷隆盛や大久保利通、公家の岩倉具視らは倒幕を朝廷に働きかけました。⑤同年12月9日、朝廷は王政復古の大号令を発し、幕府を廃止して天皇中心の政治を行なうことを明らかにしました。⑥こうして江戸幕府は滅亡しました。
⑦新政府は、徳川氏に領地の返上を要求するなど厳しい姿勢で臨みました。⑧新政府軍は江戸城を戦わずして明けわたさせました。⑨翌年には、箱館の五稜郭で旧幕府軍を降伏させました。⑩この内乱を戊辰戦争といいます。

66. The Boshin War（戊辰戦争）

I'll return the administration to the Court.
私は政権を朝廷に返すことにした。

徳川慶喜は大政奉還を行ないました。

Return your territories! Decline your official rank!
領地を返せ！
官位を辞退しろ！

慶喜への方針が示されました。

1868年1月

It's the beginning of the *Boshin* war.
戊辰戦争が始まったぞ。

この方針に旧幕府軍は反発し、鳥羽・伏見（京都）で新政府軍と戦いました。

Let's go back to *Edo*.
江戸に戻ろう。

しかし、旧幕府軍は敗れ、江戸に戻りました。

Let's capture the *Edo-jo* castle!
江戸城を攻め落とすぞ！

新政府軍は江戸を目指して進撃しました。

第4章　近代●国際社会の中の日本

江戸

I want to avoid a meaningless fight.
無益な戦いは避けたいでごんす。

Spare the life of shogun, and we will give up the *Edo-jo* castle.
江戸城を明けわたすので、将軍の命は助けてほしい。

幕臣の勝海舟は新政府軍の西郷隆盛と会談し、江戸城は戦わずして新政府軍に明けわたされました。

We'll strike down all that is on the side of the shogunate.
幕府の味方はすべて倒すぞ！

抵抗する東北の諸藩を新政府軍は次々と降伏させました。

Let's establish an independent country in *Ezo* and make a comeback.
蝦夷を独立国にして再起をめざそう！

幕臣榎本武揚と旧幕府の海軍は箱館に立てこもりました。

五稜郭

I'm beaten.
参った。

新政府軍は五稜郭の戦いで榎本らを破りました。

The new government could unify the whole country.
新政府は日本全国を統一しました。

戊辰戦争はようやく終わりました。

67. The Meiji Restoration

①In 1868, the *Meiji* government, which defeated the *Edo* shogunate, announced the Charter Oath of Five Articles and revealed the new government's political platform. ②*Edo* was renamed *Tokyo* and the new era was named *Meiji*. ③The capital was moved from *Kyoto* to *Tokyo*. ④The traditional policy was continued and Christianity and *Ikki* were banned under the rule of the five placards of the Charter Oath.

⑤The new government carried out a centralized government to realize the new political platform. ⑥It forced *Daimyo to* return their land and people to the Emperor (*Hanseki-hokan*) in 1869. ⑦Moreover, the new government put an end to *Han* and newly placed *Ken* (prefecture), and appointed prefectural government (*Fu-chiji* and *Ken-rei*) in each *Ken* (*Hai-han-chi-ken*) in 1871.

⁸The new government abolished the class system of the *Edo* period, *Shi-no-ko-sho*, and ensured the equality of all people (*Shimin-byodo*). ⁹People who used to be the classes of *No* (peasant), *Ko* (craftman) and *Sho* (merchant) were called *He-min* and could give themselves family names.

67. 明治維新

①江戸幕府を倒した明治新政府は、1868年、五箇条の御誓文を発表し、新政府の政治方針を明らかにしました。②江戸は東京と改称され、元号も新たに明治と定められました。③また、首都はそれまでの京都から東京へと移されました。④一方で五榜の掲示を出し、キリスト教や一揆を禁止するなど、従来の政策を続けようとしました。

⑤新政府は、政治方針を実現するために中央集権化を進めました。⑥まず、1869年には版籍奉還を行ない、諸大名に土地と人民を天皇へ返させました。⑦1871年には廃藩置県を行ない、藩を廃止して新たに県を置き、府知事・県令(後の知事)を任命しました。

⑧また新政府は、江戸時代の士農工商という身分制度を改め、四民平等を唱えました。⑨江戸時代に農工商の身分だった人々は平民と呼ばれるようになり、苗字を名乗ることが許されました。

68. Nation's Wealth and Military Strength

①The *Meiji* government thought Japan should build up national strength to stand against powerful foreign countries. ②The government carried out three reforms: the educational system, the military system and the tax system.

③The government tried to establish the educational system for nation's wealth and military strength. ④It issued the ordinance, *Gakusei*, in 1872. ⑤It required all people six years of age and older to receive elementary education.

⑥In 1873, the government enforced the Land Tax Reform to secure tax revenue. ⑦It imposed a 3% tax on land price and forced the owners to pay cash. ⑧Peasants suffered from this heavy land tax and rose in *Nomin-ikki* all over the country.

⑨The government launched the reform of the military

system. ⑩ In 1873, the Conscription Ordinance was
          徴兵令
enforced and obliged all males 20 years of age and
実施された   ～することを義務づけた 男子
older to serve three years conscription.
       3年間兵役に就くこと
⑪ The government developed modern industries and
                                近代工業
carried out the encouragement of new industry.
                殖産興業

68．富国強兵

①明治政府は欧米の国々に対抗するために国力を強めるべきと考えました。②そこで、学制、兵制、税制の3つの改革を行ないました。

③まず政府は、富国強兵のために教育制度の充実をはかりました。④1872年には**学制**を公布しました。⑤学制により、6歳以上のすべての男女が小学校教育を受けることになりました。

⑥また政府は、財政収入の安定をはかるため、1873年、**地租改正**を実施しました。⑦その内容は、税率を地価の3％として所有者に現金で納めさせるというものでした。⑧地租は農民にとって非常に重い負担であったため、各地で農民一揆が発生しました。

⑨政府は兵制にも着手しました。⑩1873年、**徴兵令**が公布され、満20歳以上の男子に3年間の兵役が義務づけられました。

⑪政府は近代工業の育成にも力を入れ、**殖産興業**を進めました。

69. Civilization and Enlightenment

①Japan aggressively took in Western cultures as a result of the *Meiji* government's modernization policy. ②European clothes, coats and hats became popular instead of traditional kimono. ③People began to eat meat. ④They built brick buildings, rode on coaches and jinrikisha (human-powered cart), and installed street lamps in large cities. ⑤A railroad was laid between *Tokyo* and *Yokohama* in 1872 and later between *Kobe* and *Kyoto*. ⑥The solar calendar started being used in place of the lunar calendar in 1872. ⑦Newspapers and magazines were put out in large quantities because of letterpress printing and people came to know the modern thought from Western countries. ⑧It was *Fukuzawa Yukichi* and *Nakae Chomin* that popularized such thought. ⑨*Yukichi* wrote *Encouragement of Learning*. ⑩*Chomin* translated and published *The Social Contract* by Rousseau and introduced European democracy. ⑪The introduction of European institutions and cultures changed people's lifestyle. ⑫This is called Civilization and Enlightenment.

---

69. 文明開化

①明治政府が近代化を進めた結果、日本国内に欧米の文化が盛んに取り入れられるようになりました。

②それまでの着物にかわり、洋服やコート、帽子などが流行しました。③食生活では肉食が始まりました。④大都市ではレンガ造りの建物が建設され、馬車や人力車が走り、通りには街灯がつけられるようになりました。⑤1872年には東京・横浜間に鉄道が開通し、ついで神戸・京都間にも開通しました。⑥同年、太陰暦にかわり太陽暦が採用されました。

⑦活版印刷による新聞や雑誌の発行も盛んになり、欧米から伝わった近代思想が人々の間に広まりました。⑧このような思想を広めた人物として有名なのが福沢諭吉と中江兆民です。⑨福沢諭吉は『学問のすゝめ』を書きました。⑩中江兆民はルソーの『社会契約論』を翻訳、出版し、ヨーロッパの民主主義を日本に紹介しました。

⑪このように欧米風の制度や文化が取り入れられたことにより、人々の生活様式が大きく変化しました。⑫これを**文明開化**といいます。

70. The Seikan-ron and the Seinan War

①One of the tasks of modern nations was drawing a border. ②The *Meiji* government made the Sakhalin-Kuril Island Exchange Treaty with Russia, which stated that Sakhalin belonged to Russia and *Chishima* belonged to Japan in 1875.

③In 1871, the *Meiji* government entered into Japan-Qing Amity Treaty with Qing. ④This was the first equal treaty the *Meiji* government made. ⑤In the *Meiji* government, *Saigo Takamori* wanted to open Korea by military means and to have an influence in Korea (*Seikan-ron*). ⑥Nevertheless, *Iwakura Tomomi* and *Okubo Toshimichi* insisted on prioritizing growth of national power instead. ⑦They defeated *Saigo Takamori* and he left the government. ⑧The government, however, took advantage of the Kanghwa Island Incident to enter into the Treaty of Kanghwa with Korea in 1875, and forced it

to open the country.
　　　　　開国する

⑨ *Shizoku* (former low-class samurai) rose in revolts all
　　士族　　　　　　　　　　　　　　　　　　　　反乱を起こした
over the country. ⑩ Among them, the *Seinan* war
　　　　　　　　　　　　　　　　　　　　　　西南戦争
started by *Saigo Takamori* was the largest revolt but
～によって起こされた　　　　　　　最も規模の大きな反乱
the government army suppressed it.
　　　　　　　　　　　　鎮圧した

70．征韓論と西南戦争

①領土を決めることは近代国家としての課題の一つでした。
②1875年、政府はロシアと**樺太・千島交換条約**を結び、樺太はロシア領、千島列島は日本領と**画定**しました。
③1871年、明治政府は清（中国）と**日清修好条規**を締結しました。④これは、明治新政府が結んだ初めての対等な条約でした。
⑤政府内では、**西郷隆盛**らを中心に、朝鮮に対し武力で開国を迫り、日本の影響力を強めようとする**征韓論**が高まりました。
⑥しかし、**岩倉具視**や**大久保利通**らは、そうではなく国力の充実を優先させるべきと主張しました。⑦征韓論に敗れた西郷らは政府を去りました。⑧しかし政府は1875年、**江華島事件**をきっかけに**日朝修好条規**を締結し、朝鮮を開国させました。
⑨維新改革に不満を持つ士族たちは、各地で反乱を起こしました。⑩なかでも、西郷隆盛が起こした**西南戦争**は最も規模の大きな反乱でしたが、政府軍によって**鎮圧**されました。

71. The Movement for Democratic Rights

① After *Saigo Takamori* left, *Okubo Toshimichi* took a leading part in the government. ② *Okubo Toshimichi* carried out the encouragement of new industry and was at the wheel of the country. ③ *Itagaki Taisuke*, who left the government with *Saigo Takamori*, criticized the government for the tyranny by the people from *Satsuma-han* and *Choshu-han*. ④ He required to reflect the people's will on the government and brought in the report to ask for establishing the Diet elected by the people in 1874. ⑤ This was the beginning of the movement for democratic rights.

⑥ The movement spread to all over the country. ⑦ In 1880, leaders of the movement established the association, *Kokkai-kisei-domei*, in *Osaka* and required the government to set up the Diet.

⑧ In 1881, the government was going to dispose of its

facilities in *Hokkaido* to a well-known merchant, and the people of the movement for democratic rights criticized the government strongly. ⑨The government gave up the disposal. ⑩It also issued the edict to set up the Diet in 1890.

---

71. 自由民権運動

①西郷隆盛らが政府を去った後、西郷に代わって政府の中心となったのが**大久保利通**です。②大久保利通は殖産興業を進めるとともに、国内の支配を強化していきました。③西郷とともに政府を去った**板垣退助**は、政府を薩摩・長州など一部の藩の出身者による専制政治（**藩閥政治**）だと批判しました。④そこで、国民の意見を政治に反映させることを要求し、1874年に**民撰議院設立の建白書**を政府に提出しました。⑤これが**自由民権運動**の始まりです。

⑥自由民権運動は各地に広まりました。⑦1880年には全国の自由民権運動の代表者が大阪に集まり、**国会期成同盟**を設立し、政府に国会の開設を求めました。

⑧1881年、北海道の施設を政府と結びつきの強い商人に払い下げようとする事件が起こり、民権運動派は政府を強く非難しました。⑨政府は、払い下げを中止しました。⑩また、国会開設の勅諭を下し、1890年に国会を開くことを約束しました。

72. The Constitution of the Empire of Japan and the Imperial Diet

①The *Meiji* government was getting ready to set up the Diet. ②The government wanted to establish the Constitution before setting up the Diet. ③It thought that the Constitution which made much not of human rights but of the power of the Emperor was needed to carry out nation's wealth and military strength. ④*Ito Hirobumi* went to Europe and studied the Constitution of Germany and made out a draft Constitution. ⑤The Cabinet system was adopted and *Ito Hirobumi* became the first prime minister.

⑥The Constitution of the Empire of Japan stipulated that sovereignty rested with the Emperor and gave strong power to him. ⑦The imperial Diet had two-chamber system: *Shugi-in* and *Kizoku-in*. ⑧The *Kizoku-in* consisted of the imperial family, *Kazoku*, those who were appointed by the Emperor and high-income

taxpayers. ⁹*Shugi-in* members were elected by the people. ¹⁰Nevertheless, the number of people who were eligible to vote was very small.
¹¹In this way, the public could take part in national government though there were restrictions. ¹²Japan became the first modern constitutional country in Asia.

72. 大日本帝国憲法と帝国議会

①明治政府は国会開設のための準備を進めました。②政府は、国会開設の前に憲法を制定しようとしました。③富国強兵を進めるために人権よりも天皇の権限を重視した憲法が必要だと考えました。④**伊藤博文**はヨーロッパへ留学して、ドイツ（プロイセン）の憲法を学び、憲法の草案を作成しました。⑤また、**内閣制度**が創設され、伊藤博文が初代**内閣総理大臣**に就任しました。⑥**大日本帝国憲法**は天皇を主権者とし、天皇に強い権限が与えられました。⑦**帝国議会**は、**衆議院**と**貴族院**からなる二院制でした。⑧貴族院議員は皇族や華族、天皇が任命した者、高額納税者などでした。⑨議員が選挙で選ばれたのは衆議院のみでした。⑩しかも衆議院議員の選挙権をもっていた人は、少数に限られていました。

⑪制限つきでしたが、国民が国政に参加する道が開かれました。
⑫日本はアジアで最初の近代的な立憲制国家となりました。

73. The Treaty Revision

① An important task of the *Meiji* government was revising the unequal treaties which the *Edo* shogunate made with foreign countries.
② Japan agreed on restoration of customs autonomy with the U.S. in 1878 but couldn't obtain any other countries' agreement. ③ Later, Japan took a Westernization policy and established the building, *Rokumei-kan*, and held a ball to give foreign countries the impression that Japan was a developed country.
④ In 1894, Britain agreed to negotiate with Japan to counter the Russia's movement toward the south. ⑤ The foreign minister, *Mutsu Munemitsu*, made Anglo-Japanese Commercial Treaty with Britain and succeeded in lifting exterritoriality and restoring a part of customs autonomy. ⑥ Afterward, he could revise unequal treaties with other countries.

⑦In 1911, the complete revision of customs autonomy was realized by the foreign minister, *Komura Jutaro*.
　　　　　　　　～によって実現された　　　　　　　　　小村寿太郎

73. 条約改正

①江戸幕府が諸国と締結した不平等条約の改正は、政府にとって重要な課題でした。

②1878年にアメリカとの間で関税自主権の回復で合意しましたが、他の国々の合意は得られませんでした。③その後、欧化政策をとり、**鹿鳴館**を建設し、**舞踏会**を催して、外国に日本が進んだ国であることを印象づけようとしました。

④1894年、ロシアの南下に対抗するためイギリスはついに交渉に応じました。⑤外相**陸奥宗光**によって**日英通商航海条約**が結ばれ、**領事裁判権（治外法権）**の撤廃と関税自主権の一部回復に成功しました。⑥続いて、他の諸国とも条約改正に成功しました。

⑦関税自主権の完全な回復は、外相**小村寿太郎**のもと、1911年に実現しました。

74. The Japanese-Sino War

①After the conclusion of the Treaty of Kangwa, Japan extended its influence on the Korean Peninsula and had a conflict with Qing.
②In Korea, believers of a religion, *To-gaku*, rose in revolt to reject foreigners and to call for political reform in 1894.

③Japan and Qing sent their armies to Korea on the grounds of settlement of the revolt. ④After that, Japan made war against Qing on August 1, 1894. ⑤It ended in victory for Japan.

⑥In 1895, a peace conference was held in *Simonoseki* and the Treaty of *Shimonoseki* was made between Japan and Qing. ⑦Qing recognized the independence of Korea, and it was forced to give up Liaodong Bandao and Taiwan to Japan and to pay the war indemnity.
⑧The Treaty of *Shimonoseki* increased the status of

第4章　近代●国際社会の中の日本

Japan in the international community and Japan got a
　　　国際社会で
foothold to expand into the continent. ⁹Nevertheless,
足場を得た　　～へ進出する　　　　大陸
Russia, in cooperation with France and Germany,
　　　　～と協力して
required Japan to return Liaodong Bandao to Qing.
要求した　　　　　　～に返還する
⑩Japan followed the requirement. ⑪Japan, however,
　　　　要求に従った
developed a dislike for Russia.
　　　　～への反感

74. 日清戦争

①日朝修好条規の締結後、日本は朝鮮半島へ勢力を伸ばし、清（中国）との間に対立が深まりました。

②朝鮮では、1894年に宗教（東学）を信じる人々が、外国人の排斥や政治改革を求めて反乱を起こしました（甲午農民戦争）。

③甲午農民戦争を鎮めることを口実に、日本と清は朝鮮に出兵しました。④その後、日本軍は、1894年8月1日宣戦を布告し、日清戦争が始まりました。⑤戦いは日本の勝利に終わりました。

⑥1895年、講和会議が下関（山口県）で開かれ、講和条約（下関条約）が結ばれました。⑦下関条約で清は朝鮮の独立を認め、遼東半島・台湾などを日本に譲り、賠償金を日本に支払うことが決められました。

⑧日本は下関条約で国際的な地位を高め、大陸進出の足場を築きました。⑨しかし、ロシアはフランス・ドイツと結んで、遼東半島を清に返還するよう日本に要求してきました（三国干渉）。
⑩政府は、遼東半島を返還しました。⑪しかし、日本国民はロシアへの反感を強めました。

75. The Japanese-Russo War

①Qing was defeated by a small country like Japan, so powerful countries such as Russia and Britain hunted for concessions in Qing. ②A secret society, the Boxers, protested the colonial rule by foreign countries and started a movement to reject them. ③In 1900, the Boxers surrounded embassies in Bejing and eight powerful countries including Japan sent armies there and kept it down.

④After this incident, Russia kept troops in Manchuria and expanded into Korea. ⑤Japan and Britain felt threatened and entered into Anglo-Japanese Alliance. ⑥*Uchimura Kanzo* and others protested against war but an aggressive mood was prevailing in Japan.

⑦The Japanese-Russo war broke out in 1904. ⑧Japan occupied Lushun on Liaodong Bandao and destroyed the Baltic Fleet. ⑨Nevertheless, it was the limit of

military power of Japan. ⑩Russia had the domestic
problem of a revolutionary movement. ⑪Therefore,
both countries wanted to make peace, so they
concluded the Treaty of Portsmouth in 1905.

75. 日露戦争

①清が日本のような弱小国に敗れると、ロシアやイギリスなどの列強は清での利権を漁りました。②清国内では秘密結社の義和団を中心にして、清の半植民地化に抗議し、外国勢力を追い出す運動が起こりました(義和団事件)。③1900年には義和団は北京にある各国の公使館を包囲しましたが、これに対して日本をはじめとする列強8カ国は軍隊を北京に派遣し、これを鎮めました(北清事変)。

④義和団事件後も、ロシアは満州に軍隊をとどめ、韓国へも進出しました。⑤脅威を感じた日本とイギリスは、**日英同盟**を結びました。⑥内村鑑三らは開戦に反対しましたが、日本国内では開戦ムードが高まりました。

⑦1904年、**日露戦争**が始まりました。⑧日本軍は遼東半島の旅順を占領し、**バルチック艦隊**を壊滅させました。⑨しかし、日本の戦力は限界に達していました。⑩ロシア国内でも革命運動が起こりました。⑪そのため、日露両国は講和を望み、1905年、**ポーツマス条約**が締結されました。

76. The Battle of Tsushima (日本海海戦)

> What a severe battle!
> 何て激しい戦いなんだ!

日露戦争において、多くの犠牲を出しながら、日本は旅順を陥落させました。

> That'll show you.
> どうだ!

ロシアは大艦隊であるバルチック艦隊を黒海から日本海へ出撃させました。

> We can hardly call at harbors because the shipping lane is along British colonies.
> 航路はほとんどイギリスの植民地だから、上陸できないぞ。

日英同盟を結んでいたイギリスは、ロシアにスエズ運河を通らせませんでした。

第4章 近代 ●国際社会の中の日本

> We're very tired.
> 疲れたよ。

バルチック艦隊の士気はあがりませんでした。

> The survival of Japan depends on this battle.
> 皇国の興廃この一戦にあり！

日本海軍のモチベーションは最高でした。

> Cross the face of the enemy and barrage them!
> 敵前を横切って、集中砲火を浴びせろ！

> ウルサイ！

司令官東郷平八郎の作戦も的中し、バルチック艦隊を破りました。

> Let's modernize our country like Japan.
> 日本にならって近代化を進めよう。

> Asia should obey Japan.
> アジアは日本に従うべきだ。

> Japan is a first-rate nation in the world.
> 日本は世界の一流国さ。

日本の勝利はロシア支配下の国々に希望を与えました。

一方で、日本国民に大国意識をめばえさせるきっかけにもなりました。

77. The Annexation of Korea and the Industrial Revolution in Japan

① After the Japanese-Russo war, Japan colonized Korea and placed the governing institution, *Tokan-fu*, in Seoul. ② *Ito Hirobumi* became the first *Tokan* (the chief of it). ③ Soldiers and people of Korea made a stand against the invasion and assassinated him in 1909. ④ Japan annexed Korea in 1910 and placed the governing institution, *Chosen-sotoku-fu*, and ruled it until 1945.

⑤ The *Meiji* government carried out the encouragement of new industry and modernized industry. ⑥ The Japanese industrial revolution took place around light industry and Japan exported cotton goods to Korea and China in the 1890s.

⑦ Around the Japanese-Russo war, the heavy industry sector developed in Japan. ⑧ *Mitsui*, *Mitsubishi*, *Sumitomo* and *Yasuda* grew into conglomerates which ruled the Japanese economy.

⁹There were new problems with the development of industries. ⁱ⁰Young female workers who supported the
                                                                     若い女子労働者
textile industry were forced to work long hours, and
繊維産業   ~することを強いられた
male workers were forced to do heavy work in the
男子労働者   重労働
mining industry.
鉱山業

77．韓国併合と日本の産業革命

①日露戦争後、日本は韓国の植民地化を進め、ソウルに統監府を置きました。②初代統監には伊藤博文が就任しました。③韓国の兵士や民衆は日本の侵略に抵抗し、1909年には伊藤博文を暗殺しました。④1910年、日本は**韓国を併合**し、朝鮮総督府を置いて、1945年まで支配しました。

⑤明治政府は殖産興業を進め、産業の近代化を進めました。
⑥日本では軽工業を中心に産業革命が始まり、1890年代には綿製品を朝鮮や中国へ輸出するようになりました。
⑦日露戦争前後には重工業部門が発展しました。⑧三井・三菱・住友・安田は、日本経済を支配する**財閥**に成長していきました。
⑨重工業が発展する一方、新たな問題も発生しました。⑩繊維産業を支えていた若い女子労働者は、長時間労働に従事させられ、男性労働者は鉱山業などで厳しい労働を強いられていました。

78. Modern Cultures

①Modern literature developed through the unification of the spoken and written language. ②Tsubouchi Shoyo wrote *The Essence of the Novel* in 1885 advocating realism in which the writers expressed facts and people's feelings warts and all. ③Futabatei Shimei wrote *Ukigumo* (Floating Cloud) in a colloquial style. ④Around the Japanese-Sino war, romantic literature which made much of people's emotion came on the scene. ⑤As for novels, *Higuchi Ichiyo*'s *Child's Play* (Measuring Heights) and *Mori Ogai*'s *The Dancing Girl* were famous. ⑥In poetry, *Yosano Akiko*'s *Tangled Hair* and *Shimazaki Toson*'s poem collection, *Wakana-shu* were popular.

⑦At the time of the Japanese-Russo war, naturalistic literature became at its best and *Ishikawa Takuboku* wrote *A Handful of Sand*. ⑧*Natsume Soseki* established his own literature based on individualism and wrote *Botchan* (Master) and so on.

⑨In art, Fenollosa and *Okakura Tenshin* worked hard to revive Japanese-style painting. ⑩*Yokoyama Taikan* opened up the new style of modern painting.

---

78. 近代の文化

①近代文学発展のきっかけとなったのは、話し言葉(口語)で文章を書くという言文一致でした。②1885年、坪内逍遙は『小説神髄』を著し、事実や人間の心の動きをありのままに表現しようとする写実主義を提唱しました。③二葉亭四迷は言文一致体の『浮雲』を著しました。

④日清戦争の前後になると、人間の感情面を重視するロマン主義文学が起こりました。⑤小説では『たけくらべ』の樋口一葉や『舞姫』の森鷗外がよく知られています。⑥詩歌では『みだれ髪』の与謝野晶子や『若菜集』の島崎藤村らが活躍しました。

⑦日露戦争のころには自然主義が盛んとなり、『一握の砂』の石川啄木らが活躍しました。⑧夏目漱石は個人主義に基づく独自の文学をうちたて、『坊っちゃん』などを著しました。

⑨芸術ではフェノロサが岡倉天心と協力して日本画の復興に努めました。⑩横山大観は近代絵画の新しい様式を開拓しました。

79. World War I and Japan

① In 1914, the Prince and Princess of Austria was assassinated by a Serbian young man in Sarajevo. ② Austria made war against Serbia. ③ Germany, which was allied with Austria, was on Austria's side and Britain, France and Russia were on Serbia's side. ④ Japan wanted to expand into the continent and declared war on Germany on the grounds of Anglo-Japanese Alliance.

⑤ In 1918, Germany gave in and World War I ended. ⑥ In 1919, a peace conference was held in Paris and the Treaty of Versailles was concluded. ⑦ In this peace conference, Japan got the concessions of Germany, so anti-Japanese sentiment grew in China. ⑧ Students in Beijing started an anti-Japanese movement on May 4, 1919 and it grew into a large-scale movement (*Go-Shi* movement).

⁹In Korea, members of the independence movement
                          独立運動
declared the independence of Korea on March 1,1919.
独立を宣言した
¹⁰They marched in a demonstration and it spread all
デモ行進を行なった   〜全土に広がった
over Korea. ¹¹This is called the *San-Ichi* independence
                                三・一独立運動
movement but Japan quieted it by military means.
                          鎮めた   武力で

79. 第１次世界大戦と日本

①1914年、**サラエボ**で、オーストリアの皇太子夫妻が**セルビア**の青年に暗殺されました。②これを機に、オーストリアがセルビアに宣戦布告しました。③オーストリアと同盟関係にあった**ドイツ**がこれに加わり、セルビアを支援する**イギリス・フランス・ロシア**との間で戦争が起こりました。④日本は大陸進出の好機として、**日英同盟**を理由にドイツに宣戦しました。
⑤1918年、ドイツが降伏し、第１次世界大戦は終わりました。
⑥1919年にはパリで講和会議が開かれ、**ベルサイユ条約**が結ばれました。⑦この講和会議で、ドイツ利権の日本への継承が認められたため、中国の反日感情は高まりました。⑧1919年5月4日、北京の学生が反日運動を起こし、大規模な運動へ発展しました(**五・四運動**)。
⑨1919年3月1日、朝鮮では、独立運動家が独立を宣言しました。⑩人々はデモ行進を行ない、朝鮮全土に広がりました。⑪これを**三・一独立運動**といい、日本は武力でこれを鎮めました。

175

80. The War Boom and the Rice Riot

① Europe was the battlefield of World War I, so Japan was not damaged by the war. ② Japan enjoyed an unprecedented economic boom because exports increased by a flood of orders of war supplies from Western countries. ③ The domestic machine industry and chemical industry developed because of the decrease of imports from those countries.

④ The economic boom invited price increase. ⑤ Especially, rice prices rose sharply. ⑥ In 1918, housewives in a fishing village in *Toyama* hit rice stores for cheaper rice. ⑦ With this case as a start, people all over the country stood up and hit rice stores and big shops. ⑧ This is called the rice riot. ⑨ About 700,000 people took part in it and the government kept it down by military means. ⑩ The *Terauchi Masatake* Cabinet resigned in a body to take responsibility for the rice riot.

⑪ The Great *Kanto* Earthquake struck on September 1, 1923 and *Tokyo* and *Yokohama* were destroyed by it.
関東大震災　　　　　　　　起こった　　　　　　　　　　　　　　　　　　　　　　　　　　　　　　壊滅状態となった
⑫ It also caused a heavy damage to the national economy.
　　　　　～に大きな打撃を与えた　　　　　　　　　　　　　　国内経済

80．大戦景気と米騒動

①第 1 次世界大戦はヨーロッパが主な戦場であり、日本の国土は被害を受けませんでした。②さらに、欧米諸国から軍需品の注文が殺到し、大幅に輸出が増大して、それまでにない**好景気**をむかえました。③また、欧米諸国からの輸入が減少したため、機械工業、化学・薬品工業などが発達しました。
④好景気は物価の上昇を招きました。⑤特に米価は急激に上昇しました。⑥1918 年、富山県の主婦たちが米の安売りを要求して米屋を襲いました。⑦これをきっかけに、全国各地で民衆が決起し、米屋や大商店を襲いました。⑧これを**米騒動**といいます。
⑨米騒動は約 70 万人が参加する大騒動となり、政府は軍隊を出動させてようやくこれをおさえました。⑩米騒動の責任をとって寺内正毅内閣は総辞職しました。
⑪1923 年 9 月 1 日、**関東大震災**が起こり、東京や横浜は壊滅状態となりました。⑫経済も大きな打撃を受けました。

81. The Taisho Democracy

①In the *Meiji* period, the government was carried out with officials and military men at its center. ②In 1912, *Katsura Taro* formed his cabinet and ignored the Diet, so *Ozaki Yukio* and *Inukai Tsuyoshi* started the *Kensei-yogo* movement to seek a government with the Diet at its center. ③This movement received public support and the *Katsura* Cabinet was overthrown.
④*Yoshino Sakuzo* advocated *Minpon-shugi* in which public opinion would be reflected in the government by popular election. ⑤This democratic tendency in the *Taisho* period is called *Taisho* democracy.
⑥In 1918, the president of the political party, *Rikken-seiyu-kai*, *Hara Takashi*, became prime minister and formed a real party cabinet for the first time. ⑦The second *Goken* movement began in 1924 and the president of the political party, *Kensei-kai*, *Kato*

Takaaki, formed a coalition cabinet. ⑧After that, it became a political custom for party presidents to form the cabinet.

⑨In 1925, the *Kato* Cabinet enacted the law of popular election. ⑩The peace preservation law was also enacted to crack down on communists at the same time.

81. 大正デモクラシー

①明治時代から官僚（役人）や軍人中心の政治が行なわれていました。②1912年に桂太郎が組閣をする際、議会を無視する態度をとったため、尾崎行雄や犬養毅らが中心となって議会中心の政治を求める**憲政擁護運動（護憲運動）**を起こしました。③運動は国民の支持を受け、桂内閣は倒れました。

④**吉野作造**は、普通選挙によって民意を政治に反映させるという**民本主義**を主張しました。⑤このように大正時代に起こった、民主主義の風潮を**大正デモクラシー**といいます。

⑥1918年、立憲政友会総裁**原敬**が首相となり、はじめての本格的な政党内閣が成立しました。⑦1924年に第二次護憲運動が起こり、憲政会総裁の加藤高明を首相とする連立内閣が成立しました。⑧以後、政党の総裁が内閣を組織することが政治の習わしとなりました。

⑨1925年、加藤内閣は**普通選挙法**を成立させました。⑩共産主義者を取り締まるための**治安維持法**も同時に成立させました。

82. The World Crisis and the Response of the Countries

①After World War I, the U.S. became a key player in the global economy. ②The stock market crashed on the New York Stock Exchange in 1929, banks went bankrupt and many people lost their jobs. ③This confusion became a world crisis.
④In the U.S., Franklin Roosevelt established the New Deal to increase employment through public works projects. ⑤Britain and France adopted a bloc economy and raised tariffs to force foreign goods out of their colonies. ⑥The Soviet Union, the socialist state, was carrying out a five-year plan, so it was not affected by the world crisis. ⑦Germany, Italy and Japan were pushed out of these economic blocs and suffered a serious blow.

⑧Germany had trouble paying the war indemnity of World War I. ⑨Hitler of the Nazi Party received public support. ⑩Hitler was elected to office in 1933, and German Nazis left the League of Nations and increased armaments. ⑪In Italy, the Fascist party led by Mussolini took the helm of the country and strengthened its military power.

82. 世界恐慌と各国の対応

①第1次世界大戦後、世界の経済の中心となったのはアメリカでした。②しかし1929年、ニューヨーク証券取引所で株価が大暴落し、銀行がつぶれ、失業者が街にあふれました。③この混乱をきっかけに**世界恐慌**が起こりました。

④アメリカは、フランクリン・ルーズベルト大統領がニューディール政策を打ちたて、大規模な公共事業をおこして、失業者を減らそうとしました。⑤イギリスやフランスは、関税を高くして植民地から他国の商品をしめ出す**ブロック経済**政策をとりました。⑥5カ年計画を進めていた社会主義国のソ連は、恐慌の影響を受けませんでした。⑦ドイツやイタリア、日本などは、こうした経済圏からしめ出され、深刻な打撃を受けました。

⑧ドイツは第1次世界大戦の賠償金の支払いに苦しめられていました。⑨**ナチス党のヒトラー**が国民の支持を受けました。⑩ヒトラーは、1933年に政権を握ると、国際連盟から脱退し、軍備を強化しました。⑪イタリアではムッソリーニが率いる**ファシスト党**が政権を握り、軍事力を強めました。

83. The Manchurian Incident

①The world crisis did heavy damage to the Japanese economy and it slipped deep into recession (*Showa* crisis). ②The price of farm produce decreased sharply and peasants had a hard life. ③Industrial and agrarian disputes frequently arose.
④In China, the Republic of China was founded in the Chinese Revolution led by Sun Wen in 1911, but armed factions engaged in struggle for power all over the country and it remained politically instable. ⑤After Sun Wen's death, Chiang Kai-shek became the leader of the Kuomintang Party.
⑥The Japanese army (the Kwantung army) blew up railway of the South Manchuria Railway in September 1931, made a false charge against the Chinese army and took military action. ⑦This is the Manchurian incident. ⑧The Kwantung army occupied the main part

of Manchuria and established Manchukuo in March 1932. ⑨The League of Nations sent the Lytton Commission and urged Japan to pull its troops out of Manchuria. ⑩Japan left the League of Nations to protest it.

---

83. 満州事変

①世界恐慌は日本の経済にも大打撃を与え、深刻な不況に陥りました(昭和恐慌)。②農作物の価格は暴落して農村の生活は苦しくなりました。③そのため労働争議や小作争議が激化しました。

④中国では、1911年に孫文が指導した辛亥革命で中華民国が成立しましたが、軍閥の勢力争いが各地で活発となり、政治は不安定なままでした。⑤孫文が死去すると、蒋介石が中国国民党の指導者となりました。

⑥日本軍(関東軍)は、1931年9月、南満州鉄道の線路を爆破し、これを中国軍のしわざとして軍事行動を開始しました。⑦これを満州事変といいます。⑧関東軍は満州の主要部を占領し、1932年3月には満州国をつくりました。⑨国際連盟は、リットン調査団を派遣し、日本軍の満州からの引き上げを求めました。⑩しかし日本はこれに反発し、国際連盟を脱退しました。

84. The Withdrawal from the League of Nations (国際連盟脱退)

Manchukuo was established in 1932.
満州国が1932年に建国されました。

満州事変が起こり、日本は満州（中国東北部）を占領しました。

We investigated the Manchurian incident.
満州事変の調査を行ないました。

国際連盟はリットン調査団を派遣しました。

The Manchurian incident was not Japan's self-defense.
満州事変は日本の正当防衛ではない。

Manchukuo should be under control of some countries including Japan.
満州は日本を含めた数カ国で共同管理すればよい。

リットン調査団は「日本の軍事行動は不法」とする報告書を発表しました。

日本側はこの報告書を批判しました。

第4章 近代●国際社会の中の日本

国際連盟の会議で、日本代表松岡洋右は報告書を激しく批判しました。

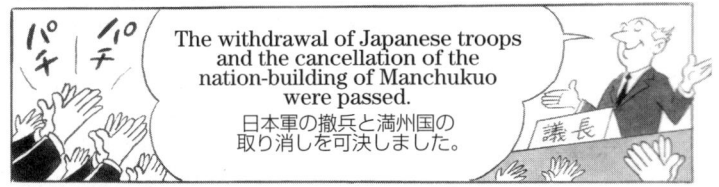

しかし国際連盟の総会は、満州国の取り消しを決定しました。

松岡洋右は国際連盟からの脱退を宣言しました。

松岡は総会の会場から退場しました。

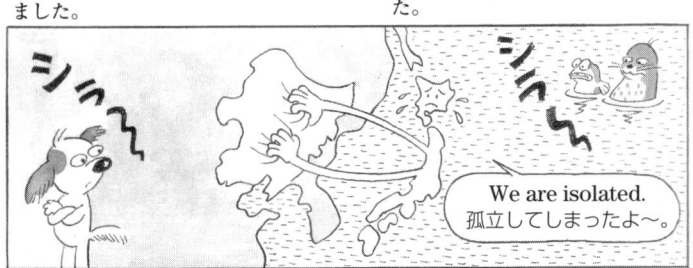

国際連盟からの脱退は、日本が世界から孤立するきっかけになりました。

85. The Rise of the Military and the Japanese-Chinese War

①In Japan, the military and nationalists began to think of overthrowing the party cabinet to invade the continent.

②The Prime Minister at that time, *Inukai Tsuyoshi*, opposed the approval of Manchukuo and wanted to settle the Manchurian Incident in negotiation with China. ③Some young naval officers were unhappy with it and assassinated him on May 15, 1932. ④This incident is called *Go-ichi-go-jiken*.

⑤On February 26, 1936, some young army officers attempted a coup d'état and attacked the office of the Prime Minister. ⑥They occupied central *Tokyo* for a while. ⑦This incident is called *Ni-niroku-jiken*. ⑧It ended in failure but the military got a bigger voice in the government. ⑨Japan concluded the agreement, the *Nichi-Doku-I-sangoku-bokyo-kyotei*, with Germany and Italy in 1937.

⑩In July 1937, the Japanese-Chinese war broke out.
　　　　　　　　　　　　　　　　　　　　　　日中戦争
⑪The Japanese army occupied Nanjing and killed many
　　　　　　　　　　　　占領した　　　南京
Chinese including women and children. ⑫The Chinese
　　　　　　〜を含む　　　　　　　　　　　　　　　　　　中国国民党
Kuomintang Party and the Communist Party formed the
　　　　　　　　　　　　　　　　　共産党　　　　　　　　　　結成した
united front, the *Konichi-minzoku-toitsu-sensen*.
　　戦線　　　　　　抗日民族統一戦線

85．軍部の台頭と日中戦争

①日本国内では軍部や国家主義者の間に、大陸侵略を進めるために政党内閣を倒そうと考え始めました。
②当時の首相犬養毅は、満州国を承認することに反対していて、中国との交渉で満州事変の解決をはかろうとしていました。
③これを不服とした海軍の青年将校らが1932年5月15日、犬養毅首相を暗殺しました。④これを五・一五事件といいます。
⑤1936年2月26日には、陸軍の青年将校がクーデターを企て、首相官邸などを襲撃しました。⑥一時は東京の中心部を占拠しました。⑦これを二・二六事件といいます。⑧クーデターは失敗に終わりましたが、軍部の政治的発言力は強くなりました。
⑨日本は、1937年にドイツ、イタリアと日独伊三国防共協定を結びました。
⑩1937年7月、日中戦争が始まりました。⑪日本軍は南京を占領、その際女性や子どもを含む多くの中国人を殺害しました（南京事件）。⑫中国では国民党と共産党が抗日民族統一戦線を結成しました。

86. The Reinforcement of the War Footing

①The war dragged on and the government muzzled the newspapers and broadcasting and censored publications to crack down on antiwar ideas.
②The National Mobilization Law was set up in 1938 and the government came to be able to mobilize the people and goods without the Diet approval. ③In 1940, almost all the political parties and groups dissolved and they were bound together into the institution, *Taisei-yokusan-kai*, so the Diet lost substance.
④The war footing impacted the lives of the people. ⑤A rationing system was introduced and people found difficulty getting basic goods. ⑥The neighborhood community associations were formed in each town and village, and everyday life of the people was controlled.
⑦In 1941, elementary school was changed into *Kokumin-gakko* and it provided militaristic education.

⁸In Korea, in the name of the policy of the *Kominka*, Japan forced people to use the Japanese language and Japanese style names (*Soshi-Kaimei*) and to visit shrines. ⁹In 1938, Japan mobilized the Korean people by the system of the *Shigan-hei-seido*.

86. 戦時体制の強化

①日中戦争が長引くにつれて、政府は新聞や放送などを統制し、出版物に対して検閲を行ない、戦争に批判的な言論や思想を取り締まりました。
②1938年には国家総動員法が定められ、議会の承認なしに、物資と国民すべてが戦争のために動員されることになりました。③1940年には、ほとんどの政党や政治団体が解散し、大政翼賛会という組織にまとめられ、議会は形だけのものになりました。④国民の生活も戦時体制の影響を受けました。⑤配給制が導入され、生活必需品が手に入りにくくなりました。⑥町や村には隣組がつくられ、日常生活は統制されました。⑦1941年には、小学校が国民学校に改められて軍国主義の教育が行なわれるようになりました。
⑧朝鮮では、皇民化の名のもとに、日本語の使用や日本式の氏名を名乗る創氏改名を強制したり、神社をつくって参拝させたりしました。⑨1938年には志願兵制度がつくられ、朝鮮の人々も戦争に動員されました。

87. Germany and World War II

① German Nazis led by Hitler ignored the Treaty of Versailles and started to invade neighboring countries. ② Germany annexed Austria and, later, Czechoslovakia, and formed a military alliance with Italy. ③ After the conclusion of a mutual nonaggression treaty with the Soviet Union, Germany made inroads into Poland. ④ Britain and France proclaimed war against Germany and World War II broke out. ⑤ In 1940, Italy took part in the war on the German side and Germany brought France to terms and began air raids on London. ⑥ Germany also occupied Greece and Yugoslavia in 1941 and subjected most of Europe to its rule. ⑦ In June 1941, Germany tore up the mutual nonaggression treaty and started to make inroads into the Soviet Union.

⑧ After the Soviet army defeated the German army in Stalingrad in 1943, the allied forces began to fight back

and brought down Mussolini and brought Italy to
terms. ⑨In May 1945, the Soviet army occupied Berlin
and Hitler killed himself, and Germany surrendered.

87.ドイツと第2次世界大戦

①ヒトラーが率いたナチス・ドイツは、ベルサイユ条約を無視して周辺諸国への侵略を開始しました。②オーストリア、チェコスロバキアを併合して、イタリアと軍事同盟を結びました。③さらにソ連と不可侵条約を結ぶと、ポーランドに侵攻しました。④これに対し、イギリスやフランスはドイツに宣戦し、第2次世界大戦が始まりました。⑤1940年、イタリアもドイツ側に加わって参戦しました。ドイツはフランスを降伏させ、ロンドンへの空襲も行ないました。⑥1941年にはギリシャやユーゴスラビアを占領し、ヨーロッパのほとんどを支配下に置きました。⑦1941年6月には不可侵条約を破ってソ連に侵攻を開始しました。

⑧1943年にソ連軍がスターリングラードでドイツ軍を破ると、連合国軍の反撃が始まり、ムッソリーニを失脚させ、同年9月にはイタリアを降伏させました。⑨1945年5月、ソ連軍はベルリンを占領し、ヒトラーは自殺してドイツも降伏しました。

88. The Outbreak of the Pacific War

①As the war dragged on, Japan got into bad terms with the U.S. and Britain. ②Japan became in a difficult position because it had depended on the U.S. for resources such as oil and ironstone. ③Japan aimed at expanding into Southeast Asia to secure them. ④Japan insisted on establishing an Asian Greater East Asia Coprosperity Sphere. ⑤Japan made inroads into northern French Indochina in 1940. ⑥In that year, Japan established the alliance, the *Nichi-Doku-I-sangoku-domei*, with Germany and Italy, and the treaty, the *Ni-So-churitsu-joyaku*, with the Soviet Union in 1941. ⑦After that, the Japanese army entered into southern French Indochina.

⑧As a punishment for it, the U.S. and Britain banned exports of oil to Japan and imposed an economic blockade by ABCD-*hoijin* (America-Britain-China-Dutch

Line) against Japan. ⑨Therefore, the Japanese military wanted to make war against the U.S. and Britain but the *Konoe Fumimaro* Cabinet negotiated with the U.S. to avoid the war, but in vain. ⑩In October 1941, when a military man, *Tojo Hideki*, became Prime Minister, war became inevitable.

~に対して　日本の軍部
~と戦争する
近衛文麿内閣　~と交渉した　避ける
しかし、うまくいかなかった　軍人
東条英機　首相　避けられない

88. 太平洋戦争勃発

①日中戦争が長期化するにつれ、日本はアメリカやイギリスとの関係が悪化しました。②石油・鉄鉱石などの資源を主にアメリカからの輸入に頼っていた日本の立場は苦しくなりました。③日本は、東南アジアに進出して資源を獲得することを目指しました。④そして、アジア民族だけで栄えようとする「**大東亜共栄圏**」の建設を主張しました。⑤1940年、フランスの植民地であった**インドシナ北部**に侵攻しました。⑥日本は同年、ドイツ・イタリアと**日独伊三国同盟**を結び、1941年にはソ連と**日ソ中立条約**を結びました。⑦さらに、日本はフランス領インドシナ南部にも軍を進めました。

⑧こうした日本の動きに対し、アメリカ・イギリスは日本への石油輸出禁止や、**ABCD包囲陣**による経済封鎖を実行しました。⑨これに対し、日本の軍部はアメリカやイギリスと開戦しようと考え、反対に**近衛文麿**内閣は戦争を避けるために日米交渉を続けましたが交渉での解決は実りませんでした。⑩1941年10月に軍人の**東条英機**が首相になると、開戦は決定的となりました。

89. The Wartime Life of the People

① On December 8, 1941, the Japanese army landed on British Malay Peninsula and the navy made a sneak attack at Pearl Harbor. ② Japan declared war against the U.S. and Britain, and the Pacific War broke out. ③ Japan said it was a war for the establishment of the Greater East Asia Coprosperity Sphere and Asian liberation from Western rule. ④ Nevertheless, Japan occupied Singapore, Burma, Philippine and Indonesia and didn't recognize their independence.

⑤ At first, Japan succeeded in extending the front in Southeast Asia but it was defeated in the Battle of Midway Island in June 1942 and in the Battle of Guadalcanal in August. ⑥ The tide of war changed and the allied forces launched a large-scale counterattack. ⑦ In Japan, people and commodities were all mobilized. ⑧ College students also went off to war by *Gakuto-*

shutsujin in 1943. ⑨Japan brought in a large number of people against their will from Korea and China to secure manpower. ⑩In July 1944, the allied forces occupied Saipan and attacked Japan from the air.

89. 戦時下の国民生活

①1941年12月8日、日本の陸軍はイギリス領マレー半島に上陸し、海軍はハワイの真珠湾を奇襲しました。②日本は、アメリカ・イギリスに宣戦布告して、太平洋戦争が始まりました。③日本軍は戦争の目的を「大東亜共栄圏」の建設にあるとして、アジアの諸民族を欧米諸国の植民地支配から解放すると謳いました。④しかし、シンガポール・ビルマ（現在のミャンマー）・フィリピン・インドネシアなどを占領しても、諸国の独立を認めませんでした。

⑤開戦してしばらくは東南アジアの戦線拡大に成功していた日本軍でしたが、1942年6月にミッドウェー海戦で敗れ、同年8月にガダルカナル島での攻防戦に敗れました。⑥すると戦局は一変し、連合国軍の反撃が本格化しました。⑦日本国内では、人も物資も戦争に動員されました。⑧1943年には学徒出陣が始まり、大学生も戦地に送られました。⑨労働力確保のため、朝鮮や中国からも多くの人々を強制連行しました。⑩1944年7月にサイパン島が連合国軍に占領されると、日本本土を空襲しました。

90. The Potsdam Declaration and the End of the Pacific War

① From 1944, B-29 bombers made air raids on Japan. ② In March 1945, *Tokyo* suffered a random attack by fire bombs and was turned into complete burnt-out ruins. ③ About 100,000 people fell victim to it. ④ The allied forces landed on *Okinawa*. ⑤ Japan battled against them, mobilizing even junior high school students and female students, but it was defeated. ⑥ More than 120,000 people fell victim to it.

⑦ In July 1945, Truman of the U.S., Churchill of Britain and Stalin of the Soviet Union had a conference in Potsdam and announced the Potsdam Declaration to demand Japan's unconditional surrender. ⑧ Japan, however, rejected the demand and the U.S. dropped atomic bombs over *Hiroshima* on August 6, 1945 and *Nagasaki* on August 9 in order to bring the war to a rapid conclusion. ⑨ These atomic bombs took more than 300,000 victims. ⑩ On August 8, the Soviet Union tore up the Soviet-Japanese Neutrality Treaty and joined the war. ⑪ Japan decided to accept the Potsdam Declaration on August 14.

---

90. ポツダム宣言と太平洋戦争の終結

① 1944年からはB29大型爆撃機による日本本土への空襲が本格化しました。② 1945年3月、東京が焼夷弾による無差別攻撃を受け(東京大空襲)、東京は焼け野原となりました。③ 約10万人が犠牲になりました。④ 連合国軍は沖縄に上陸しました。⑤ 日本軍は中学生や女学生まで動員して戦いましたが敗れました。⑥ 12万人以上の住民が犠牲になりました。

⑦ 1945年7月には、アメリカのトルーマン、イギリスのチャーチル(のちアトリー)、ソ連のスターリンがドイツのポツダムで会談し、日本の無条件降伏を求めるポツダム宣言を発表して日本に呼びかけました。⑧ しかし、日本はこれに応じず、アメリカは戦争の早期終結を目的に、1945年8月6日に広島、9日に長崎に原子爆弾を投下しました。⑨ あわせて30万人以上の犠牲者を出しました。⑩ 8月8日にはソ連が中立条約を破棄して参戦しました。⑪ 日本政府は、8月14日にポツダム宣言受諾を決めました。

91. Postwar Japan

①The U.S. led allied forces were stationed in Japan. ②The Japanese government carried out the government under the eye of the General Headquarters of the Allied Forces (GHQ), whose commander was MacArthur. ③The GHQ put a lot of reforms into effect in order to abolish militarism and establish a democracy. ④The military was disbanded and war leaders were punished as war criminals. ⑤The Emperor denied being a descendant of God (the Humanity Declaration).

⑥The GHQ made a draft of the Constitution and the government amended it. ⑦The Constitution of Japan went into effect on May 3, 1947. ⑧It has three broad principles: Sovereignty with the people, Respect for fundamental human rights and Pacifism.

⑨The United Nations was organized in 1945, but the world was divided into two parts: free countries and socialist countries (the Cold War). ⑩Japan made the Treaty of San Francisco with 48 countries in 1951 and the Japan-Soviet Joint Declaration with the Soviet Union in 1956. ⑪Therefore, Japan could join the United Nations.

社会主義国　冷戦
サンフランシスコ平和条約
日ソ共同宣言
加盟する

91. 戦後の日本

①日本には、アメリカを中心とする連合国軍が進駐しました。
②マッカーサーを最高司令官とする**連合国軍最高司令官総司令部(GHQ)**のもとに日本政府が政治を行ないました。
③GHQは軍国主義を廃絶し、民主主義を定着させることを目的に、多くの改革を実行しました。④軍隊は解散され、戦争の指導者は戦争犯罪人として処罰されました。⑤天皇は、神の子孫であることを否定しました(**人間宣言**)。
⑥憲法はGHQの案をもとに改正されました。⑦**日本国憲法**が1947年5月3日より施行されました。⑧それは国民主権、基本的人権の尊重、平和主義を三大原則とするものです。
⑨1945年に**国際連合**がつくられましたが、世界は自由主義国(西側)と社会主義国(東側)に二分していました(**冷たい戦争[冷戦]**)。⑩1951年に日本はアメリカなど48カ国と**サンフランシスコ平和条約**を結び、1956年には**日ソ共同宣言**が出されました。⑪これをもって日本は国際連合に加盟しました。

監修者

中西康裕 (なかにし やすひろ)
1957年大阪府生まれ。
関西学院大学・同大学院を経て、現在、関西学院大学文学部教授。
文化歴史学科にて日本古代史を研究。古代国家の成立過程や古代の基本史料六国史の検討、河内の歴史の解明を主に研究している。
主な著書に『続日本紀と奈良朝の政変』(吉川弘文館)ほかがある。

Gregory Patton (グレゴリー パットン)
1965年米国ワシントンD.C.生まれ。
コロラド大学卒業後来日、英会話学校講師を経て、現在、公立小・中学校外国語講師。

※本書は、2004年10月に小社より刊行された『らくらくわかる!英語対訳で読む日本史』を加筆・修正し、新書化したものです。

じっぴコンパクト新書　020

意外に面白い! 簡単に理解できる!
英語対訳で読む日本の歴史
～The Japanese History with simple English

2008年 9月3日　初版第1刷発行
2011年12月9日　初版第8刷発行

監修者	中西康裕＋Gregory Patton
発行者	村山秀夫
発行所	実業之日本社

〒104-8233　東京都中央区銀座1-3-9
電話(編集) 03-3535-2393
　　(販売) 03-3535-4441
http://www.j-n.co.jp/

印刷所……………大日本印刷
製本所……………ブックアート

©MY PLAN 2008 Printed in Japan
ISBN978-4-408-10740-0(学芸)
落丁・乱丁の場合は小社でお取り替えいたします。
実業之日本社のプライバシー・ポリシー(個人情報の取扱い)は、上記サイトをご覧ください。
本書の一部あるいは全部を無断で複写・複製(コピー、スキャン、デジタル化等)・転載することは、法律で認められた場合を除き、禁じられています。また、購入者以外の第三者による本書のいかなる電子複製も一切認められておりません。